WORLD BANK WORKING PAPER NO. 146

Integrity in Mobile Phone Financial Services

Measures for Mitigating Risks from Money Laundering and Terrorist Financing

Pierre-Laurent Chatain
Raúl Hernández-Coss
Kamil Borowik
Andrew Zerzan

THE WORLD BANK
Washington, D.C.

World Bank Working Papers are published to communicate the results of the Bank's work to the development community with the least possible delay. The manuscript of this paper therefore has not been prepared in accordance with the procedures appropriate to formally-edited texts. Some sources cited in this paper may be informal documents that are not readily available.

The findings, interpretations, and conclusions expressed herein are those of the author(s) and do not necessarily reflect the views of the International Bank for Reconstruction and Development/The World Bank and its affiliated organizations, or those of the Executive Directors of The World Bank or the governments they represent.

The World Bank does not guarantee the accuracy of the data included in this work. The boundaries, colors, denominations, and other information shown on any map in this work do not imply any judgment on the part of The World Bank of the legal status of any territory or the endorsement or acceptance of such boundaries.

The material in this publication is copyrighted. Copying and/or transmitting portions or all of this work without permission may be a violation of applicable law. The International Bank for Reconstruction and Development/The World Bank encourages dissemination of its work and will normally grant permission promptly to reproduce portions of the work.

For permission to photocopy or reprint any part of this work, please send a request with complete information to the Copyright Clearance Center, Inc., 222 Rosewood Drive, Danvers, MA 01923, USA, Tel: 978-750-8400, Fax: 978-750-4470, www.copyright.com.

All other queries on rights and licenses, including subsidiary rights, should be addressed to the Office of the Publisher, The World Bank, 1818 H Street NW, Washington, DC 20433, USA, Fax: 202-522-2422, email: pubrights@worldbank.org.

ISBN-13: 978-0-8213-7556-3
eISBN: 978-0-8213-7557-0
ISSN: 1726-5878   DOI: 10.1596/978-0-8213-7556-0

Cover image by Diego Britos.

Library of Congress Cataloging-in-Publication Data

Integrity in mobile phone financial services : measures for mitigating risks from money laundering and terrorist financing/Pierre-Laurent Chatain ... [et al.].
    p. cm. -- (World Bank working paper ; no. 146)
    Includes bibliographical references.
    ISBN 978-0-8213-7556-3 -- ISBN 978-0-8213-7557-0 (electronic)
  1. Home banking services--Security measures. 2. Electronic funds transfers--Security measures. 3. Cellular telephone systems--Security measures. 4. Commercial crimes--Prevention. I. Chatain, Pierre-Laurent, 1961- II. World Bank.
    HG1711.I58 2008
    332.1'70684--dc22

                                 2008013191

Contents

Foreword vii

Acknowledgments ix

Abbreviations and Acronyms xi

Executive Summary xiii

1. **Introduction** 1
   Background 1
   Objective 2
   Scope and Target Audience 3
   Geographical Coverage 3
   Outline 6

2. **m-FS Growth Potential and Concerns** 7
   m-FS Offers Unique Economic Development Potential 7
   m-FS Development Demands a Convergence of Stakeholder Incentives 9
   Perceived ML and TF Risks and the Case for Regulation 11
   Market Access and the Case for Regulatory Balance 14

3. **Analyzing and Responding to ML and TF Risks: Observations
   of Applied Practices** 17
   New Challenges to Old Risk Analysis Methods 17
   New Framework for Risk Analysis 18
   ML and TF Risks Inherent in the Four m-FS Service Categories 20
   ML and TF Risks External to m-FS Service Categories 29

4. **Applying FATF Recommendations to m-FS** 33
   Observed Mitigation Responses and their Consistency with FATF
   Recommendations 33
   Application of AML and CFT Standards to All m-FS Providers 41

5. **Conclusions and Policy Recommendations** 47
   Conclusions 47
   Policy Recommendations and Issues for Consideration 48

Appendix A. m-FS Growth 55

Appendix B. Types of m-FS and m-FS Services Observed in Fieldwork .. 57

Appendix C. Mitigation Measures for m-BSA 61

Appendix D. Mitigation Measures for m-Money 67

Appendix E. The Financial Action Task Force (FATF) 69

Appendix F. Overview of m-FS Risk Identification and Mitigation 71

Glossary 73

Bibliography 75

Author Biographies 79

LIST OF TABLES

1. The Four Identified Risk Factors 13
2. Possible ML and TF Risks and Observed Control Measures for m-BSA 25
3. Concurrent Use of m-FS 30
4. Observed m-FS Licensing and AML and CFT Compliance Requirements 32
5. Most Relevant FATF Recommendations for Risk-Based Consideration 41
6. Factors Contributing to Growth of m-FS 56
7. m-fINFO in Visited Jurisdictions 57
8. m-BSA in Visited Jurisdictions 58
9. m-Payments in Visited Jurisdictions 58
10. m-Money in Visited Jurisdictions 59
11. Observed Limits on m-FS Transactions, USD (2007) 64

LIST OF FIGURES

1. Convergence of Stakeholders' Incentives Results in m-FS Growth 10
2. Mobile Financial Information Services (m-fINFO) 20
3. Mobile Bank and Securities Accounts (m-BSA) 21
4. Mobile Payment Services (m-Payments) 26
5. Mobile Money Services (m-Money) 27
6. Concurrent Use of m-FS 30
7. Soaring Market for Mobile Connections and SMS 55

LIST OF BOXES

1. m-FS Increases Access to Financial Services 8
2. Suspicious Activities Using Mobile Phones: The Case of Korea 14
3. Framework for Risk Analysis 19
4. Risk-based Determination of Transaction Limits: The Case of Korea 24

  5. Collaboration through Regulatory Dialogues 31

  6. IT Supervisory Core Group at a Central Bank. 32

  7. Guidelines Designed by Financial Institutions. 39

  8. Non-face-to-face Risk Mitigation Responses: The Case of South Africa. 62

  9. Customer Profiling Systems for AML and CFT 63

10. Korean Rules for Detecting m-BSA Suspicious Transactions 65

Foreword

A key pillar to sustainable development is expanding access to finance. Until recently, no one had envisaged that mobile phones could be such a powerful medium to achieve this objective. Private sector initiatives in utilizing mobile technologies to facilitate payments have successfully brought financial services to the doorsteps of billions of unbanked poor around the world. Today, almost half the world owns a cell phone and an estimated 1.4 billion will use cell phones to remit money domestically and across borders by 2015. The promise of mobile phone financial services lies in their delivery platform. Mobile phones are unrestrained by the infrastructural and cost requirements that have traditionally hindered banks and others from reaching the impoverished.

In order that mobile technology can facilitate access to finance for the poor, policymakers, faced with emergence of new and non-traditional service providers and changing market structures, are challenged to create an enabling environment for the sustainable growth of mobile financial services. This includes the design of a balanced regulatory framework that both supports innovation and mitigates risks that threaten its development. Concerns on money laundering and terrorist financing risks have made identifying the actual risks an even more daunting task. The need to comply with international standards to mitigate these risks has further created market fears that the cost of regulatory compliance could be prohibitive, creating a disincentive to expand mobile financial services and, resultantly, undermine development.

This Working Paper, based on fieldwork in a variety of markets, is the first of its kind to specifically evaluate these concerns. Initial results have substantiated findings in recent analyses that market practices to mitigate prudential risks often coincide with those for money laundering or terrorist financing. Consequently and contrary to perceptions, mobile service providers' risk mitigation measures are consistent with international AML/CFT standards. Possibilities of sharing of information among bank and non-bank mobile service providers offer potential to reduce compliance costs, an important factor in the expansion of mobile financial services to promote access to finance and development. Greater cooperation among regulators of financial services and TelCos to facilitate the convergence of regulations of financial services and payments systems can further reduce regulatory cost.

It is our hope that the new information, findings, analyses and proposals in this paper will contribute to policymakers' efforts to promote a safe and sound regulatory regime. The right balance of regulations and cost to manage risks will provide the required enabling environment for mobile phone financial services to facilitate access to the poorer segments of society, and ultimately, foster sustainable development.

Michael Klein
Vice President Finance and Private Sector Development, The World Bank
Chief Economist, IFC

Acknowledgments

This publication was written by Pierre-Laurent Chatain (Task Team Leader), Raúl Hernández-Coss, Kamil Borowik, and Andrew Zerzan of the World Bank. The authors are especially grateful to Latifah Merican-Cheong, Director, Financial Market Integrity, World Bank, for her guidance and comments in producing this Working Paper and to Jose de Luna and Kamil Borowik, World Bank, for conceptualizing the initial work in this area following the World Bank-DFID 2006 International Conference on Migrant Remittances and Access to Finance.

The peer reviewers for the paper were Thorsten Beck, Sameer Goyal, Jean-Claude Hillion of the Bank of France, Samuel Munzele Maimbo, Mark Pickens of CGAP, Thomas Rose, and Emiko Todoroki. Their comments, discussion, and follow-up sharpened the paper and we thank them greatly. These inputs were further enhanced by the insight of the Payment Systems Unit of the World Bank.

The authors would like to thank our World Bank colleagues for their insight and feedback during the drafting process, in particular that of Jean Pesme and Wameek Noor of Financial Market Integrity.

We also benefited from consultation with the Financial Systems Unit including Augusto de la Torre (now Chief Economist of Latin America and the Caribbean Region), David Scott, and Joon Soo Lee; Massimo Cirasino and Carlo Corazza of the Payment Systems Unit; JaeHoon Yoo of the Capital Markets Unit; Maryse Gautier, Portfolio Operations Manager and Acting Philippines Country Director; and Ethan Weisman, Lead Economist for Brazil.

The support of the Finance and Private Sector colleagues in each of the visited regions was also important to our work. We would especially like to thank those working in Latin America and the Caribbean Region, the East/South Africa Region, and the East Asia/Pacific Region.

The help of our support staff, Thelma Ayamel, Oriana Bolvaran, Nicolas de la Riva, Maria Orellano, Susana Coca, Priscilla Infante, and Elena Mekhova, has been critical from start to finish. The labors of our editor, Sarah Dotson, are also appreciated.

The authors would also like to express their gratitude to the Consultative Group for the Poor (CGAP), including Tim Lyman and Denise Leite Dias, for their collaboration on several of the country visits and during the drafting process when informal discussions on fieldwork analysis helped make the paper stronger.

The World Bank-International Finance Corporation (IFC)-CGAP Mobile Banking Group. Bridgit Helms, Peer Stein, Patricia Wycoco, Luc Vaillancourt, and others in the IFC gave industry insight that was crucial. Additionally, we would like to show our appreciation for the work of Jose de Luna, Financiera Rural (Mexico), Hennie Bester of Genesis Analytics (South Africa), and David Porteous.

The authors want also to thank the International Monetary Fund's Financial Integrity Group for their input, in particular, Steve Daw.

The fieldwork for this paper was done in seven markets: Brazil, Hong Kong SAR of China, Macao SAR of China, Malaysia, the Philippines, South Africa, and South Korea. The time of all those met in these locations will not be forgotten. Although the following list is not nearly exhaustive, we would like to highlight some of the organizations and people without whom we could not have produced this paper:

Brazil: Ministerio de Justicia (Departamento de Recuperação de Ativos e Coopereção Juridica Internacional); Conselho de Controle de Atividades Financeiras (COAF); Banco Central do Brasil; ANATEL; Caixa Econômica Federal; Banco do Brasil; Bradesco; Banco Itaú; HSBC; Banco Real; ABN AMRO; Lemon Bank; Unibanco; Banco Cacique; Association of Brazilian Commercial Banks; Claro; Vivo; Oi; Tim; Paggo Participações; Antenor Pereira Madruga Filho, Chief solicitor (Office of the Advocate-General); Pinheiro Neto Advogados; and Antonio Gustavo Rodrigues, President, COAF.

Hong Kong SAR of China: The Government of the Hong Kong Special Administrative Region (Narcotics Division, Security Bureau); Hong Kong Police Force (Narcotics Bureau); Hong Kong Monetary Authority; Joint Financial Intelligence Unit; Office of the Telecommunications Authority (OFTA); Security Bureau; Commercial Crime Bureau; HK Association of Banks; SCB; HSBC; Bank of China; DBS; Standard Chartered Bank; Philippine National Bank, Hong Kong Branch and PNB Remittance Center; and Mr. Nelson Cheng, former Superintendent, Security Bureau.

Macao SAR of China: Macao Monetary Authority; Macao Financial Intelligence Office; Macao Telecommunications Company (CTM); Bank of China, Macau Branch; and Banco Nacional Ultramarino.

Malaysia: Bank Negara Malaysia; Malaysian Communications and Multimedia Commission; Malayan Banking Berhad (Maybank); Bank Islam Malaysia Berhad; CIMB Group; Association of Banks in Malaysia (ABM); Maxis Communications Berhad; Mobile Money International; and Dato' Zamani Abdul Ghani, Deputy Governor, Bank Negara Malaysia.

Philippines: Bangko Sentral ng Pilipinas; Department of Finance; Anti-Money Laundering Council Secretariat; Asian Development Bank; USAID Philippines, Microenterprise Access to Banking Servcies (MABS); Globe Telecom and G Xchange; Smart Communications; BancNet; Banco de Oro Universal Bank; Asia United Bank; Rural Bankers Association of the Philippines; Nestor A. Espenilla, Jr., Deputy Governor, Bangko Sentral ng Pilipinas; Pia Bernadette Roman, Technical/Bank Officer, Bangko Sentral ng Pilipinas; John Owens, Microenterprise Access to Banking Services (MABS); Mr. Vicente Aquino, Executive Director, AMLC; and Paolo Baltao, G Xchange.

South Africa: South African Reserve Bank; South African Financial Intelligence Centre; National Treasury; Committee of Central Bank Governors Payment Systems Project; Competition Commission; Payments Association of South Africa; The Banking Association South Africa; South Africa Post Bank; Absa; Standard Bank of South Africa Limited; First National Bank; BANKSERV; Fundamo; Smartcom; FinMark Trust; WIZZIT and South African Bank of Athens; Timothy Hobden, Genesis Analytics; Professor Louis de Koker, Advisor to the South Africa Anti-Money Laundering Council; and Brian Richardson of Wizzit.

South Korea: Bank of Korea; Financial Supervisory Service; Korean Financial Intelligence Unit; Korea Securities Research Institute; Kookmin Bank; Korea Federation of Banks; Korea Institute of Finance; Ministry of Information and Communication; SK Telecom; LG Telecom; KTF; and In Seok Kim and the IT Supervision Team of the Financial Supervisory Service. The authors would also like to express their appreciation to the Executive Director in the office for Korea at the World Bank and the staff of the office for their active support.

Abbreviations and Acronyms

[NB: Abbreviations and acronyms are defined in the glossary]

AML	Anti-Money Laundering
ATM	Automatic Teller Machine
CDD	Customer Due Diligence
CFT	Combating the Financing of Terrorism
DNFBP	Designated Non-Financial Businesses and Professions
FATF	Financial Action Task Force
FIU	Financial Intelligence Unit
FSRBs	FATF-styled Regional Bodies
IT	Information Technology
KYC	Know-Your-Customer
m-FS	Mobile Financial Services
m-fINFO	Mobile Financial Information Services
m-BSA	Mobile Bank and Securities Account
m-Money	Mobile Money
m-Payments	Mobile Payment Services
ML	Money Laundering
RSP	Remittance Service Providers
SAR	Special Administration Region
SIM	Subscriber Identification Module
SMS	Short Message Service
STR	Suspicious Transaction Report
TelCo	Mobile Telecommunications Company
TF	Terrorist Financing
VAS	Value-Added Service

Executive Summary

*T*his working paper explores strategies to identify and manage potential money laundering *(ML) and terrorist financing (TF) risks in mobile financial services (m-FS).* Using field-work in seven economies[1] as a basis, the paper provides guidance on the best means of assessing perceived versus actual ML and TF risks, then identifies specific measures to mitigate the actual risks. The paper concludes with recommendations that aim to promote a regulatory balance to foster an enabling environment for business while minimizing ML and TF risks that hinder its sustainability.

Mobile phones hold great potential to become a common way of conducting financial transactions on a global scale in the near future. Billions of people around the world use mobile phones to communicate, and the technology has even become accessible to low-income and remote populations in recent years. For the nearly three billion people who currently do not have bank accounts, mobile technology offers new means for them to access financial services. Policymakers, bank and non-bank financial service providers, and regulators all have reason to support m-FS development.

Despite the development potential of m-FS, distinctive risks concern observers in affected service markets. These perceptions merit urgent attention because m-FS providers may fall outside anti-money laundering (AML) and combating the financing of terrorism (CFT) controls generally adhered to by traditional financial institutions. In order to balance perceptions against the fear of over-regulation, which can damage business, actual rather than perceived risks need to be identified.

A service-based approach rather than a provider-led approach is more effective in assessing actual ML and TF risks for m-FS. The lines differentiating financial providers in the banking, telecom, credit card, and mobile commerce sectors have become blurred. With the crossover of mobile phone and payment systems operators into the financial services sector, potential risks more likely depend on the characteristics and complexity of service provided than on the service provider. A service-based approach offers greater flexibility to identify and diminish actual risks and is more favorable to creating an equal playing field for all providers of all types.

In order to analyze ML and TF risks and suggest effective risk mitigation practices, the four major types of m-FS need to be analyzed separately. The four core services of m-FS are mobile financial information (m-fINFO), mobile bank and securities account (m-BSA), mobile payment (m-Payments), and mobile money (m-Money). The services often work simultaneously and, in some instances, one acts as a foundation for the others. Also, the less the service models have in common with traditional financial service models, the more their associated risks, and their potential for financial inclusion increase.

The paper identifies four risk factors in m-FS and appropriate mitigation responses. The risk factors are anonymity, elusiveness, rapidity, and poor oversight. Anonymity is the risk of not knowing a customer's actual identity, and it can be diminished through enhanced

---

1. Brazil, the Philippines, Hong Kong SAR of China, Macao SAR of China, South Africa, Republic of Korea, and Malaysia.

Know-Your-Customer procedures and identification tools. Elusiveness is the ability to disguise mobile transaction totals, origins, and destinations. It can be diminished through transaction limits and enhanced customer profiling, monitoring, and reporting. Rapidity is the speed with which illicit transactions can occur. Its risk is checked by flagging certain types of transactions and managing risks of third-party providers. The fourth type of risk is poor oversight, which can be mitigated by transparent guidelines on mobile services, clearer licensing, regulation of providers, and effective risk supervision within bank and non-bank m-FS providers.

Overall, the observed mitigation responses reflected in the working paper are consistent with international AML and CFT standards, and current Financial Action Task Force (FATF) standards address the most prominent m-FS risks. There is no need to expand the FATF 40+9 Recommendations because they provide an appropriate framework to mitigate these emerging risks. The working paper, however, highlights specific FATF Recommendations that jurisdictions could consider adopting to mitigate the identified risks. For example, non-bank providers of financial services, such as TelCos, should be considered as "Financial Institutions," as defined by FATF. However, the scope of AML and CFT obligations with which TelCos' should comply ought to be determined using a risk-based approach.

Applying the FATF 40+9 Recommendations through a risk-based approach that is service-specific appears to be the most suitable method for implementing AML and CFT without overly burdening development efforts. Using this method, authorities have the discretion to waive requirements based on their analysis of risk exposure. Policy actions should be focused on whether current AML and CFT standards have been assessed through a service-based approach, then properly and fully implemented.

Fieldwork showed that many m-FS providers were already conducting business in ways that are consistent with FATF standards. This implies that application of such standards does not constitute a barrier to business practices. Evidence from the field indicates that good business practices and AML and CFT measures are compatible so successful implementation of risk-based measures is possible without overburdening new m-FS businesses. Such controls do not impede financial innovation and may contribute to sustainable growth.

Policy Recommendations are addressed to different stakeholders from both public and private sectors.

- *Policymakers* are encouraged to recognize the development potential of m-FS and formally recognize that m-FS providers are subject to AML and CFT laws.
- *Financial Intelligence Unit (FIU)* and *Law Enforcement* authorities should develop technology and clear rules and guidelines to monitor m-FS providers.
- *Sector regulators* are encouraged to improve inter-sectoral collaboration to effectively follow developments in converging industries.
- *Supervisors* should be aware that potential m-FS risks should be given the same attention as other financial channels.
- *Bank and non-bank m-FS providers* are encouraged to collaborate with authorities to facilitate a safe, pro-business environment with self-regulation of the m-FS industry.

Finally, building on the FATF's work in the area of new technologies, the paper provides further interpretation that could be used by the FATF for future work.

CHAPTER 1

Introduction

Background

Mobile phones affect the lives of billions of people around the globe, including the poor. Changing mobile technology has revealed opportunities and allowed nearly three billion people without bank accounts (Christen, Rosenberg, and Jayadeva 2004) to access financial services. Mobile phones have provided an unprecedented opportunity for financial development and access, and are set to become a common tool for conducting financial transactions in the near future.

The private sector is responding to this great opportunity by developing mobile financial services (m-FS). Banks, mobile phone operators, and other non-bank institutions have developed financial transaction services that are available in industrialized[2] and, increasingly, in developing countries. Among the services are domestic and international money transfers; deposits and withdrawals; bill and retail payments; payroll services, loan disbursement; repayments and stock exchange trading; and even electronic currencies. The growth of these services depends on the presence of a viable business model, customer demand, and an enabling business environment.

Governments face the challenge of shaping a safe and sound business environment that is favorable to financial innovation and compliant with international standards. Policymakers and regulators have expressed concerns about consumer protection, information

---

2. In the United States alone, six of the nation's 10 biggest banks rolled out mobile financial services starting last spring, and the rest are expected to make it a standard offering by mid-2008. See Epper Hoffman, "Mobile Banking: Where's the Business Case?"

security, and similar issues in the use of mobile technology. Work is being done internationally to respond to the possible risks inherent in the use of technology for financial services delivery and intermediation (Basel 2001a; FATF 2006b). These responses can have beneficial or detrimental impacts on development of new technologies and innovative financial services, thereby expanding or limiting access to finance.

Concerns have been raised about possible misuse of mobile technologies for criminal purposes.[3] Mobile phones are used by billions of people around the world to communicate, including criminals and terrorists.[4] New mobile phone financial services may be susceptible to use in ML and TF activities. Given the development potential of these services, it is worthwhile to identify, measure, and lessen potential risks. By providing tools and recommendations to address ML and TF risks, there is a greater likelihood that the technology will be adopted in compliance with international standards.

The World Bank is committed to promoting the development of new technologies that expand access to finance and to enhancing financial market integrity. Since 2002, the Financial Market Integrity unit has been dedicated to the fight against ML and TF. It supports client countries with technical assistance and compliance assessments of international standards as part of the Financial Sector Assessment Program (FSAP). The unit also conducts policy development work aimed at identifying areas that are particularly vulnerable to financial abuse (Chatain 2004).

Discussions at the 2006 Second International Conference on Migrant Remittances[5] pointed out a gap in research on the role of mobile phones for financial inclusion and corresponding regulatory implications, which this paper begins to address.[6] The paper also builds on outcomes of the Conference and the efforts of others in the World Bank Group, namely the International Finance Corporation (IFC) and the Consultative Group to Assist the Poor (CGAP), as well as international organizations such as UK Department for International Development (DFID), the FATF, and the Bank for International Settlements (BIS).

Objective

This working paper seeks to promote mobile phone use as a means of expanding access to financial services through increased understanding of ML and TF vulnerabilities, risk mitigation strategies, and consistency with the international standards. It provides guidance

---

3. m-FS can also enhance measures to deter and disrupt illicit activities, making the technology double edged, holding potential for both criminals and police.

4. Police investigations have established that the terrorist attacks have been conducted using mobile phones as a trigger to explosives (in Madrid in 2005 and London in 2006) demonstrating that the technology is being embraced by terrorists. With the growth of m-FS, there are heightened concerns that mobile phones could be used to finance terrorism as well.

5. Organized by the World Bank and the UK Department for International Development (DFID) in London on November 13–14, 2006. For more information, see www.financelearning.org/remittances2006.

6. Mobile platforms were identified in the World Bank's Bilateral Remittance Corridor Analysis as a convenient, cheap, and safe way to transfer migrant remittances. See De Luna, Hernández-Coss, Borowik, and Lagi (2006).

on how to assess potential ML and TF risks and offers a balanced approach to implementing mitigation measures.[7] The paper's specific objectives are:

- To provide authorities and the private sector with knowledge, tools and examples in a new service-based approach that identifies, assesses, and mitigates ML and TF risks of m-FS provision.
- To assist improvements of countries' AML and CFT regimes by providing examples and recommendations on regulatory approaches. Particular emphasis is placed on oversight and supervision of financial and non-financial institutions such as mobile-phone providers (TelCos) and remittance service providers (RSPs).

Scope and Target Audience

Recognizing the potential of mobile phones to expand access to financial services, this paper concentrates on the AML and CFT aspects of mobile communications. Fieldwork was conducted[8] to gain an understanding of the use of mobile phone technology and business features of financial services offered by bank and non-bank financial institutions.

The study focuses on issues that are *unique* to m-FS such as ML and TF risk factors and means of internal control.[9] The many forms of accessing financial information and performing transactions through a mobile phone go under different names, but the term m-FS is used in this paper for simplification purposes.[10]

This working paper is designed to be accessible to a wide range of m-FS stakeholders. All of the following will find suggestions for m-FS development: policymakers (ministries of finance, science, and technology; central bankers; and telecommunications and financial regulators); FIUs; international AML and CFT standard-setting bodies; and private sector banks and non-bank financial institutions (commercial and rural banks, microfinance institutions, and telecommunications and RSPs).

Geographical Coverage

This working paper is based on research and discussions with industry, policymakers, and regulators. Fieldwork included interviews with public sector banking and telecommunication regulators, FIUs, Central Banks, and Ministries of Finance and Telecommunications;

---

7. Recent evidence suggests that an effective AML and CFT regime can both mitigate ML and TF risks while simultaneously facilitating development. Bester and others (forthcoming), "Implementing FATF Standards in Developing Countries and Financial Inclusion."

8. The team worked closely with CGAP, which has published a note on balanced regulatory regimes and non-traditional methods of accessing financial services. The two jointly visited three jurisdictions in their fieldwork. See Lyman, Pickens, and Porteous (2008).

9. Many of the ideas developed here can be applied to other non-traditional methods of accessing financial services. However, this analysis focuses on mobile platforms such as WAP and text messaging for m-FS.

10. These include m-banking, new payment methods, branchless banking, wireless banking, wireless payments, and others.

private sector TelCos, credit card companies, law firms, financial institutions, NGOs, and micro-finance institutions; and donor countries. The interviews provided the study team with information to propose policy recommendations. Fair representation from both developing and developed countries was intended to give insight on the varying conditions under which m-FS exists.[11]

The Philippines

Since 2001, the Philippines has been at the forefront of developing m-FS and is one of the first countries to provide m-FS on a large scale. Developments have been driven by two mobile providers[12] and include national and cross-border remittance transfer mechanisms. The Central Bank has played an active role in creating an enabling environment for these new services and the country has demonstrated a strong commitment to implementing an AML and CFT regime that allows financial inclusion. The Philippine case provides an example of AML and CFT regulations that does not impede the development of m-FS.[13]

South Africa

Development of m-FS in South Africa is relatively recent and has been driven by South Africa's goals to implement policies that expand access to finance while complying with AML and CFT standards.[14] South Africa responded to the fast-growing m-FS market by playing a leading role in implementing AML and CFT standards in sub-Saharan Africa and designing rules that are favorable to access to finance.[15]

Brazil

Many Brazilian financial services are provided by banking correspondents.[16] Brazil has been at the forefront of developing mobile phone payment services by credit card companies. As in many developing countries, widespread mobile phone use for financial services is still at early stage, but recent increases in mobile phone use by the low-income population[17] have prompted authorities to develop incentives for a safe and sound m-FS regulatory regime.

---

11. Examples of other countries with emerging m-FS include: Kenya, Thailand, Poland, India, Japan, some of which have been studied by CGAP, DFID, and Vodafone. See: http://cgap.org/portal/site/Technology/policy/diagnostics/.

12. Smart and Globe Telecommunications (through its subsidiary G-Xchange), one of the first non-bank mobile financial service providers.

13. Bester et al., "Implementing FATF Standards."

14. South Africa joined the FATF in 2003 and held the presidency in 2005/6.

15. The region has faced challenges in making the financial regulatory framework conducive to expanding access to finance. South Africa worked to make the framework both effective and friendly to financial inclusion.

16. Non-bank entities, such as retail stores, bakeries, and lottery houses provide basic banking services on behalf of branches of licensed banks.

17. Interviews conducted by the study team indicate that there are currently 105 million mobile phone users out of a population of 190 million. As a comparison, there are approximately 40 million bank account holders.

Hong Kong Special Administration Region (SAR) of China

In Hong Kong SAR of China, online financial services are more popular than m-FS. However, due to the unique, high-volume market for cross-border mobile remittances to the Philippines, the area is an interesting reference point for remittance sending countries. With the increasing potential of mobile phones as a transfer channel, the Hong Kong FIU has conducted ML and TF risk assessments of m-FS.

Macao SAR of China

Macao SAR of China has a developed Internet financial services market, a developing m-FS market, and strict processes in place to initiate m-FS and issue SIM cards.[18] The AML and CFT regime is still in development, but mobile phones are already examined in suspicion of money laundering activities.[19] The monetary authority is drafting electronic banking regulations to emphasize internal risk management practices that will create a safe environment for development of new payment methods and services, including m-FS.

Malaysia

In Southeast Asia, mobile phone usage has increased tremendously. Though still in an early stage of m-FS growth, authorities have proactively responded to ML and TF vulnerabilities by introducing regulations that promote new payment system mechanisms and enhance AML and CFT regimes.[20] Following the case of the Philippines-Hong Kong SAR of China remittance corridor, new mobile-phone cross-border remittance products have been developed to serve the Malaysia-Philippines and Malaysia-Indonesia remittance corridors.

The Republic of Korea

Mobile phones are already a popular means of conducting financial transactions[21] in Korea. Unlike in other countries, some providers offer international transfers through mobile phones. Moreover, Korea is globally distinctive because a quarter of all stock trades are conducted through m-FS. Additionally, TelCo and financial sector regulators have agreed on mutual responsibilities in overseeing m-FS, and the Korean FIU has identified typologies for criminal mobile phone usage.

---

18. For example, a customer must have a bank account, go in person to a bank branch, identify him or herself, fill in a form, and receive an e-banking ID and password. A letter is then issued by the bank so the customer can obtain a SIM from the mobile provider. A copy of this letter is also retained by the provider.

19. These have been analyzed by the local FIU in the framework of Suspicious Transaction Reports.

20. Malaysia was assessed for AML and CFT by the Asia-Pacific Group on Money Laundering in May 2007.

21. There are 2.5 million users of m-FS.

Outline

This paper is arranged into five chapters. The m-FS categories crosscut the chapters, serving as a reference point in the analysis of observed risks and mitigation responses, as well as for the conclusions and policy recommendations. In addition to this introductory chapter:

- Chapter 2 explores the link between the economic development potential of m-FS, ML and TF risk management techniques, and the convergence of stakeholder incentives that has sparked m-FS growth. It discusses the perceived risks associated with m-FS and calls for recognition of perceived versus real risks and their mitigation.
- Chapter 3 shows the recent developments in m-FS business models and in risk-based approaches to AML and CFT. It introduces a new risk and service-based framework for measuring ML and TF risks in the respective m-FS service categories. It then discusses the actual risks associated with each service category as well as measures observed in field visits to mitigate them.
- Chapter 4 addresses the characteristics of TelCos and non-bank providers as financial service providers. The chapter then discusses FATF's AML and CFT international standards per m-FS service category, their applicability, and whether the standards adequately address relevant risks.
- Chapter 5 concludes the paper and makes policy recommendations to the key stakeholders: policymakers and legislators; FIUs and law enforcement; sector regulators and supervisors; banks and other financial institutions; non-traditional m-FS providers; and self-regulating TelCo industry organizations. It also proposes new ideas for FATF consideration.

m-FS Growth Potential and Concerns

The following section examines the potential of m-FS growth and the need for AML and CFT regulation. It looks at the economic development potential within markets served by m-FS; the convergence of the stakeholder incentives driving m-FS growth; ML and TF risk perceptions and the need for a balanced approach to assessing and addressing them; and the promotion of financial services access in safe and sound enabling environments.

m-FS Offers Unique Economic Development Potential

Low-income people have limited access to traditional financial systems. Factors that limit access include high service costs, prohibitively long travel distances to bank branches and ATMs, and negative perceptions of financial service providers.[22] A recent World Bank report calls on stakeholders to expand access to financial services (World Bank 2007). It also suggests that limited financial access perpetuates economic disparity and potentially results in long-term demotivations for both working and saving.

As mobile technology becomes more widespread both geographically and within societies, m-FS is likely to expand. The global dispersion of the mobile telephone has increased substantially in the past few years. Moreover, in 2006 mobile phones became the first communications technology to have more users in the developing world than the developed world (GSMA 2006a), with more than 60 percent of all subscribers located in developing countries (ITU 2007). m-FS systems can be incorporated into existing mobile phone network

---

22. Bester and others (forthcoming). See also World Bank Bilateral Remittance Corridor Analysis at www.amlcft.org.

Box 1: m-FS Increases Access to Financial Services

The cost of providing m-FS is generally lower than that of traditionally delivered financial services. In South Africa, for example, the cost of the typical envelope of monthly transactions is 30 percent lower if performed through the leading mobile provider than the standard banking system (Ivatury and Pickens 2006) so more people can afford to access it. Additionally, m-FS are not impeded by geographic barriers that hinder access to traditional banking services.

Although m-FS depends on access to mobile phone and wireless coverage, both are more widespread than traditional banking infrastructures. Traditional bank access points, ATMs, and bank branches are far less prevalent in the developing than developed world, but wireless access is not (ITU 2006). The infrastructure gap that has conventionally hindered banking access in developing countries could be circumvented by the existence of wireless networks with much deeper demographic penetration. The recent success of m-FS in the Philippines (a country of over seven thousand islands) may very well be a result of its island geography and represents the potential m-FS have in other countries, like Indonesia, Maldives, Kenya, and Brazil, where geography thwarts access to financial services.

The diagram shows demographic penetration in a sample of high, middle and low income countries of traditional financial access points (ATMs and bank branches) per 100,000 people to the percent of the population able to receive a mobile signal. The mobile coverage presented here is based on a sample of 47 low and middle income, and 12 high income countries. An estimated 80 percent of the world's population had mobile coverage in 2006 and that percentage will rise to 90 percent by 2010 (GSMA 2006b).

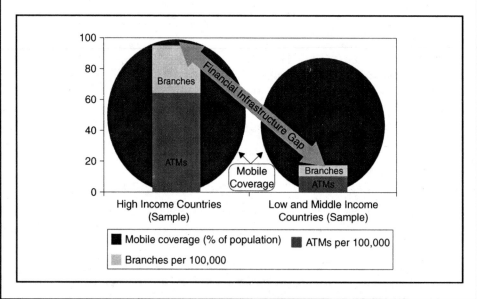

Source: Authors' calculations based on ITU (2005) and World Bank (2006).

technology, making it less demanding on infrastructural requirements than traditional branch or ATM banking. By many accounts, the potential for development leapfrog effects presented by mobile phones is unprecedented, and its soaring expansion will likely spell greater opportunities for m-FS and complementary technologies.

m-FS differs from other electronic means of accessing financial services because the technology is flexible and often more available to users. This includes regular telephone banking with bank personnel or automated bank systems using touch-tone phones to perform transactions or accessing account information through an expensive fixed-line connection. It is also distinct from Internet banking that requires an Internet connection and a computer. m-FS is carried over electronic and automated mobile messaging communications platforms such as SMS or application standards such as wireless application protocol. Neither telephone nor Internet banking offers the inherent flexibility of movement of m-FS.

The advantage of m-FS has been evident since its inception. Low infrastructural requirements; competitive advantages like low costs, increased convenience, and small transactions amounts; security features; and the ability to make cross-border remittances are all likely to promote worldwide expansion of m-FS. The key reasons for the increase in m-FS provision in the pioneer developing country, the Philippines, may be the same incentives witnessed in other countries—use of the existing widespread pre-paid mobile phone communication and text messaging systems; strong demand for financial services from the people without access to banks and financial services; strong political will to expand access to financial services to the poor and rural regions of the country; and the need to overcome geographical constraints. (The Philippines is an archipelago of 7000 islands, which makes infrastructure development difficult and costly.)

m-FS Development Demands a Convergence of Stakeholder Incentives

As observed in the jurisdictions studied, the development of m-FS requires a convergence of incentives among multiple stakeholders. Policymakers and financial and TelCo regulators and institutions all coordinate to different degrees. Banks and non-banks alike seek to capitalize on the opportunity to address the customer needs of increased access to financial services, increased convenience, and reduced service time and costs. Figure 1 illustrates the convergence of incentives.

Policymakers are motivated to support m-FS by its prospects for financial inclusion, transparency, and private sector development. They are likely to find the great potential to bridge the infrastructure and cost gaps that hinder financial service access as encouragement to support m-FS. Also, the probability that m-FS improves the traceability of financial transactions to prevent malfeasance and reinforce institutional integrity could help stir their support. Moreover, fieldwork indicates that m-FS is seen as a method to advancing innovation in financial and payment infrastructures and to promoting competition,[23] all of which contribute to the frequent policy objective of private sector growth.

TelCos benefit from expanded m-FS because it is an indirect revenue generator. The value-added nature of m-FS enhances the attractiveness of wireless service and, as a result, increases product demand.[24] This can be seen by the sizeable boost m-FS brings to text messaging revenues. Another important incentive to TelCos is the great decrease in customer turnover (also known as "churn"), which is a significant challenge to operators in an increasingly competitive market (Trucano 2006). Adding to this is the possibility that TelCos

---

23. This was mentioned repeatedly by policymakers interviewed in the visited jurisdictions.

24. The new financial service could deepen the existing market as customers use their phones more and the usefulness of mobile phones increases beyond person-to-person communication.

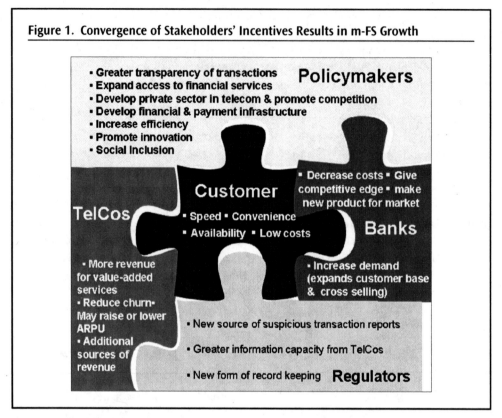

Figure 1. Convergence of Stakeholders' Incentives Results in m-FS Growth

Source: Authors' data 2008.

could sell bulk airtime to financial institutions in order to attract customers and create additional sources of revenue for both themselves and financial institutions.

TelCo operators may also directly benefit from m-FS by the addition of a new product to their line of services. In cases where m-FS is provided with little or no financial institution involvement, TelCos may take the leading role in development and sale of a financial product. This enables them to expand beyond their core business and into the financial sector. The potential to diversify product lines may present significant incentives and facilitate m-FS development.

Financial institutions have the incentive to expand their business through m-FS. As in the case of TelCos, m-FS offers new business opportunities for many financial institutions. It expands customer reach and offers greater access to products such as remittance transfers, which may prompt existing customers to increase their use of services (Todor 2007). The low infrastructure costs of m-FS also save bank resources typically needed to develop new markets (Porteous and Wishart 2006). In fact, recent evidence from the Philippines has shown that a typical bank branch transaction costs the bank $2.50, while an m-FS transaction only $0.50 (Asian Banker 2007). Among other benefits, the decrease in labor-intensive tasks offers potential gains in productivity. A study from Brazil suggests that a financial institution expected its productivity level to increase 50 percent by introducing m-FS (ABA). Such savings may translate to financial institutions being able to offer new products that are otherwise too costly to offer to the low-income market.

Regulators support m-FS because of its potential for enhanced customer protection, prudential risk mitigation, and transparency through formalization. In order to discourage the use of the informal financial sector,[25] regulators promote the use of m-FS because it provides customers with the same services but within a regulated environment. Informal services sidestep regulated and traceable channels and so run the risk of permitting ML, TF, and other criminal activities (Butler and Boyle 2003). The ability to trace and monitor transactions is central to AML and CFT efforts, so m-FS is good news to regulators who seek methods to formalize unregulated transactions without causing economic harm. m-FS offers many of the same benefits (efficiency, speed, convenience and low cost) of underground services without going under the radar of regulators.

m-FS meets customer demands for convenience, speed, availability, and low cost. m-FS often functions beyond the standard business hours of traditional banks so is more convenient and accessible. It also offers a significant time savings, particularly in areas where travel time to the nearest financial institution is considerable. In some locations, the use of traditional financial services is hindered by illiteracy and negative perceptions. m-FS does not require users to fill out of forms or interact with bank personnel, thus bypassing such impediments. In cash-based economies, the introduction of m-FS reduces exposure to theft of cash and has the potential to reduce the total volume of cash-based transactions. The costs are also significantly less than traditional methods of sending money, which is especially beneficial for those sending and receiving migrant remittances.[26]

Perceived ML and TF Risks and the Case for Regulation

The Perceived ML and TF Risks

m-FS is often perceived as posing distinctive risks in comparison with traditional ways to channel financial services.[27] The following section presents the perceptions of distinctive risks[28] identified by the study team prior to fieldwork. The main concerns identified include unknown identity; false identification; smurfing; transaction speed; phone pooling and delegation; and regulation of providers.

> ▨ *Unknown Identity.* For some, the greatest ML and TF concern is the lack of information on the identity of the m-FS user (Ehrenfeld and Wood 2007a). The possibility of hiding one's identity benefits criminals and terrorist financiers (Schott 2006). Unlike traditional financial service forms, m-FS typically does not require face-to-face interaction with financial service providers, including during the process of opening new

---

25. Money transfers are unregulated, but often faster and cheaper than traditional methods. See World Bank BRCA: www.amlcft.org.

26. A typical wire transfer from Hong Kong SAR of China to the Philippines costs twenty times more than an m-FS transaction. See Teves (2007).

27. While this section addresses the perception of risk, Chapter 3 assesses the actual risks.

28. The meaning of *distinctive risk* here is critical. For example, when conducting a money laundering operation, criminals could use a mobile phone to instruct bank personnel to make a transaction. This does not represent a distinctive risk for mobile phones because the same activity could easily be done through a fixed line telephone. Therefore the risk is not *distinctive* to mobile phones.

accounts. Moreover, it is conceivable that a transaction could be performed without a single name attached to it. If such perceptions are accurate, this lack of customer information would create a safe haven for money launderers or terrorist financiers.

▪ *False Identification.* Forged documentation used to evade detection is perceived as a serious risk in m-FS. The requirements to attain a mobile phone are often very different than those to open a bank account. Some observers point out that terrorist financiers and money launderers use aliases or third party names and information, even from the deceased (Krebs 2007). Alternately, the mobile phone may be passed off to terrorists and money launderers by those sympathetic to their efforts. Furthermore, mobile phone theft is a concern in the case of terrorists or money launders stealing a third-party's phone and using it to transfer money in the hopes of it going undetected (Krishna 2006).

▪ *Smurfing.* In banking, smurfing refers to the splitting of a large financial transaction into multiple smaller transactions (each of which is below a minimum limit above which banks report financial transactions) precisely to evade scrutiny by regulators or law enforcement (Wikipedia 2007). m-FS is perceived to be more vulnerable to smurfing because it hides the entire sum of money being transferred as small, less conspicuous amounts. Second, it is easier to "layer"[29] the funds, or hide their illicit origins through complicated movements. As m-FS is substantially cheaper than traditional financial services, the ability to increase layering and reap the rewards is greatly enhanced.

Small transactions originating from multiple accounts may go undetected. Another fear is that criminals may receive funds from multiple senders. In TF, multiple supporters could easily send small amounts of cash to a terrorist group through their mobile phones and the small sums would be less apparent to authorities. In ML, the multiple senders would work towards illicit fund "integration," in which criminals bring laundered funds into one account and mix it with "clean" money to make it less recognizable (Demetis and Dyer 2006).

▪ *Transaction Speed.* The fact that transactions can be performed quickly, virtually anytime and anyplace, is perceived to be a boon to terrorist financiers and money launderers. This new means of access to transferring funds both within and outside jurisdictions from, in the case of ML, and to, in the case of TF, criminal organizations poses problems. In the words of one observer, "the mobile person-to-person payment service provider [enables] not only South American or Filipino migrant workers to avail themselves of their m-Payments service, but perhaps also drug traffickers or supporters of al Qaeda, Hamas, and Hezbollah in the United States, who wish to send money to the Middle East, or to each other all over the world" (Ehrenfeld and Wood 2007a).

▪ *Pooling and Delegation.* Mobile phone pooling and delegation is perceived as an ML and TF risk. Pooling occurs when mobile phones are shared among many individuals

---

29. The three stages of money laundering are placement, layering, and integration. Placement is where the criminal puts ill-gotten gains into the legitimate financial system. Layering is where the funds are moved around in order to complicate tracing and ultimately hide its origins. Integration is where the money incorporated into the legitimate economy by purchase of assets, such as real estate or securities (Schott 2006).

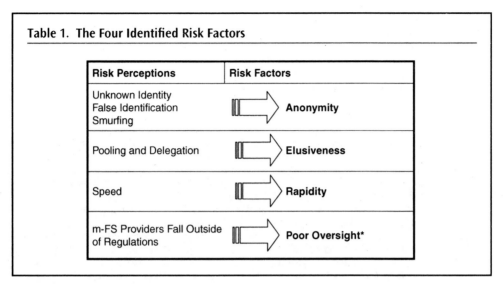

Table 1. The Four Identified Risk Factors

Risk Perceptions	Risk Factors
Unknown Identity False Identification Smurfing	Anonymity
Pooling and Delegation	Elusiveness
Speed	Rapidity
m-FS Providers Fall Outside of Regulations	Poor Oversight*

Source: Authors' field observations 2008.
*Poor oversight is not an inherent risk but can exacerbate existing inherent risks.

in poor communities. In cases of ML and TF, the initiator's identity is hidden by the registered owner of the mobile phone. The custom of delegating mobile phone use, on the other hand, is more prevalent among the wealthy, wherein an agent operates the mobile phone on behalf of the owner (Chipchase 2007). Either practice hides the originator of a transaction.

■ *m-FS Providers Fall Outside of Regulations.* There is apprehension over the fact that m-FS providers fall outside of the regulations to which other financial service institutions must adhere. AML and CFT controls, which are standard practice among traditional financial institutions such as banks, insurance companies, and securities traders, are not being fully followed by non-traditional financial service providers. For example, a TelCo's primary business is voice communication and mobile phone value-added services, not m-FS. As a result, their m-FS may not fall under a safe AML and CFT regulatory regime.[30] Even if the TelCo is itself compliant with such controls, partner entities such as retail outlets or agents and third-party billing processors may not be. Also, the TelCo or its partners may not be fully trained or aware of AML and CFT protocols and are therefore less able to effectively use them. Such gaps are thought to permit criminals and terrorists to hide their actions from law enforcement.

The Four Factors Behind the Perceived Risks

The perceived risks stem from four factors: anonymity, elusiveness, rapidity, and poor oversight. Although these factors will be discussed further, Table 1 relates them to the perceived risks discussed earlier.

---

30. Based on fieldwork.

Box 2: Suspicious Activities Using Mobile Phones: The Case of Korea

The Korean FIU (KoFIU) receives Suspicious Transaction Reports (STRs) on financial transactions performed through a variety of channels, including m-FS. The following are highlights of KoFIU's successful resolutions of suspicious m-FS activities.

■ *Cyber-Gaming Case:* A person used stolen personal information to participate in an illegal online gambling game. He hired foreign employees and used an accomplice to deposit the winnings into the Korean banking system by way of m-FS and other electronic methods. The accomplice's activities were flagged based on the suspicious nature of the international transactions. The accomplice did not offer an adequate explanation when questioned by the financial institution. An STR was filed to KoFIU that prompted an investigation by the National Police Agency's anti-terrorist cyber center.

■ *Cross-Border Remittance Case:* A person used a fake name to open several accounts and register with authorities as a Chinese national. He received large amounts of money over a short period of time from China. The money had been sent by many unspecified sources. He then withdrew the money and conducted the transactions through electronic means, including m-FS. KoFIU noted the suspicious nature of the activity and contributed their analysis to the investigation conducted by law enforcement.

■ *Swindling investment fund case:* A person founded a fraudulent financial consulting firm that tricked investors by guaranteeing high returns on investments in futures and stocks. Unwitting clients sent huge amounts of money through m-FS and other electronic channels. Financial institutions flagged suspicious deposits and withdrawals of an employee of the firm. KoFIU then analyzed the available data and notified the National Police Agency.

The use of mobile phones in suspicious activity seems to be growing. One method to measure this is to count the times the word "mobile" is mentioned in STRs. Of the 24, 149 STRs filed in 2006, 750 mentioned "mobile," whereas 808 mentioned it in the first six months of 2007 alone.

Note: The increasing number of seemingly mobile-related STRs is not conclusive proof that criminal activity in the Republic of Korea is moving toward mobile phone technology. It does, however, offer evidence that m-FS needs to be included in suspicious activity analysis.
Source: Korean Financial Intelligence Unit 2007.

Some perceptions have seemingly been substantiated by recent criminal cases of depositing, withdrawing, and transferring illicit funds through m-FS. The cases shown in Box 2 illustrate how the use of mobile phones for financial transactions creates ML and TF risks if not adequately managed. Fund transfer, foreign currency exchange, and remittances are all affected.

Market Access and the Case for Regulatory Balance

Concern on the opposite side of the spectrum is that regulation is unnecessary, impedes financial access and, ultimately, hampers economic development.[31] Policymakers could be reluctant to pass AML and CFT regulations that specifically target m-FS, and, as such, might

---

31. Such concerns can stem from policymakers interested in forwarding financial access to the poor and the private sector advocating business interests among others.

threaten economic development. Additionally, it is argued that such legislation is ineffectual in the fight against TF and ML.[32]

AML and CFT regulations that do not recognize local conditions may hinder efforts to expand financial access (Isern and others 2005). Regulations that ignore the often stark differences in market environment and institutional capacity within and between countries could make for an inefficient preventive regime. Recent evidence (Bester and others, Forthcoming) suggests that such obstacles are fully avoidable granted that policymakers modify their specifications according to local necessity in order to be realistic, flexible, and driven by a risk-based analysis in their approach to AML and CFT regulations.

AML and CFT regulation can be made to complement financial access and inclusion (Bester and others, Forthcoming). This can be achieved by close collaboration among banks, TelCos, and other stakeholders during the design process of the regulatory regime. In this way, policymakers could recognize best practices in implementation while preventing unnecessary or harmful measures. Also, close collaboration between the private sector and government on AML and CFT issues could motivate collaboration on other issues. AML and CFT effectiveness could lead to greater confidence in the market and to greater stability, investment, and overall development.[33]

Conversely, countries lacking effective AML and CFT regimes may face detrimental effects to both economic development and customer protection. In terms of economic development, a solid regulatory regime mitigates risk for service providers. This underpins investor confidence and could enhance service providers' market reputation. For consumers, the obligation of service providers to comply with minimum AML and CFT requirements brings transparency and differentiates them from criminals.

Policymakers need to identify the different risks within each m-FS business model and among service providers (financial and non-financial). Going forward, the study team concludes that it is necessary to define a new method of ML and TF risk analysis that addresses the perceived risks and responds to the need for a balanced regulatory approach (Hernández-Coss 2007). Such categorization, as proposed in Chapter 3, is required to recognize actual risks and practical mitigation techniques.

---

32. AML and CFT legislation must be followed-up by implementation. Based on analysis of AML and CFT compliance assessments, the team has observed that many low capacity countries and jurisdictions have not fully implemented AML and CFT legislation; capacity is a factor in this.

33. The Matrícula Consular, which is issued by Mexican consular authorities in the United States, has facilitated access and permitted financial services to ID undocumented users (Hernández-Coss 2005).

CHAPTER 3

Analyzing and Responding to ML and TF Risks: Observations of Applied Practices

This chapter presents risk analysis for m-FS categorized by the services a provider offers rather than by the type of provider (bank or TelCo). The rationale behind a service-based approach is explained first. Next, the mitigation responses observed in the fieldwork are presented. These measures include a variety of regulatory, supervisory, and enterprise risk management practices that will be of particular interest to policymakers, regulators, and the private sector in countries that are at the onset of developing m-FS.

New Challenges to Old Risk Analysis Methods

Traditional classification of m-FS business models by provider type is not as useful as a service-based approach for identifying and mitigating ML and TF risks. In the past, m-FS has been categorized according to the type of provider, for instance, a bank, a TelCo network, or joint venture (Porteous 2006; Wishart 2006). However, the type of provider does not necessarily determine their capacity to mitigate risks. For example, a bank is assumed to have mechanisms above and beyond those of other m-FS service providers that reduce their risk of exposure to ML and TF. Yet evidence from fieldwork and FATF, FSRB, World Bank, and IMF evaluations of AML and CFT demonstrates that this is not always the case.

A service-specific risk-based approach allows for more appropriate design and application of AML and CFT measures. Services can be provided by multiple entities in various sectors (banking, telecommunications, remittances, among others) that change rapidly and often become even more sophisticated and require increasingly complex mitigation strategies. In recent years, the international community (FATF, BIS, and others) has advocated the use of risk-based analyses to determine the necessary level of regulatory controls.

A risk-based approach allows flexibility, ensuring that policies are appropriately tuned to a particular situation (FATF 2007; Isern and others 2005). Risk mitigation techniques should take into account the category of service, customer profile, and the market.

A rules-based approach is problematic compared to a risk-based approach because it can be cumbersome and prevent financial service access when not specifically designed for the jurisdiction where it is applied. Rules-based approaches may strictly and uniformly apply controls that might not be necessary in certain environments (FATF 2007; Porteous 2006). For instance, a stringent rules-based approach can prevent the poor from accessing m-FS merely by assuming that identity verification needs to be done in person.[34] In a risk-based model, however, this problem can be overcome through one of several alternative means, including: biometric identification (voice recognition), cross-checks with a third party system of customer-provided information, or even customer profiling.

The recent convergence of services and providers in the financial sector requires a new framework for regulation, supervision, and risk analysis. The use of mobile phones for financial services has brought many new players to the formerly exclusive financial services sector. With the rapid development of technology, mobile phones were identified by non-bank providers as an opportunity to meet their customers' needs. Quite rapidly, multiple actors including banks, TelCos, payment companies, and money transfer operators engaged mobile phones as a means to offer a broader range of financial products. The lines that divided bank from TelCo, retail agent from teller, and financial and non-financial services have been blurred both in and around the m-FS context. And it is because of this interaction among financial and non-financial providers that there is need for a new framework for risk analysis.

New Framework for Risk Analysis

Regulatory frameworks did not anticipate the impact of technology, financial innovation, and the presence of multiple providers on the development of m-FS in most jurisdictions visited. Even in jurisdictions where regulations governing electronic finance exist, the use of m-FS has not been anticipated. This initially left a number of new providers, especially non-banks, outside the regulatory framework. As multiple providers interacted to deliver financial services, it became more difficult to understand and evaluate the risks involved.

During the fieldwork, four types of m-FS that may be built on top of each other were identified. m-FS are often initially offered in the form of financial information services (m-fINFO). Such services can evolve to have or may have originally included access to bank and/or securities' account services (m-BSA). In other markets, m-FS can incorporate payment services (m-Payment). Most recently, a service has been developed to provide the customer with the ability to store value and convert it into currency (m-Money).[35]

---

34. The approach may have more impact in a country where geographical distance typically prohibits face-to-face authentication of customer identity.

35. Definitions and labels of these terms vary worldwide but the functions could be grouped into these categories.

Different m-FS may demonstrate varying levels of anonymity, elusiveness, and rapidity risks. Fieldwork suggests that the level of these risks depends on the modalities of business models employed. As such, they may vary from business to business even within the same jurisdiction. A framework for analyzing key risks may facilitate regulators' efforts of case-by-case reviews of proposed m-FS business models. Anonymity, elusiveness, and rapidity have been identified as key risk categories inherent to business models employed. Investigation of inherent m-FS risks is an important focus of this paper and is explored in depth in the next section and in Appendixes C and D.

Investigation of inherent m-FS risks need to be complemented with an analysis of external risk factors such as the level of oversight in a given jurisdiction. Risk factors are associated with the overall quality of the regulatory and supervisory environment, the AML and CFT regime, and other exogenous conditions. If these combined conditions are deficient, they can create a market with poor oversight, an external risk factor that is not intrinsic to the service. Box 3 illustrates a framework for analyzing inherent and external risks of m-FS. It also provides a hypothetical example of a jurisdiction with elusiveness and anonymity risks, and an example in which m-Money, in particular, deserves heightened attention.

Box 3: Framework for Risk Analysis

Inherent Risk Factors: A service- and provider-based analysis of: anonymity, elusiveness and rapidity

External Risk Factors: A jurisdiction-by-jurisdiction analysis of regulation and oversight.

	Inherent Risk Factors			*External Risk Factors*		
	Anonymity	**Elusiveness**	**Rapidity**	**Poor Oversight**		
m-fINFO	%	%	%	*Low*	*Medium*	*High*
m-BSA	Allocation of risk factors according to characteristics of business models			Assessment of oversight capacity and AML and CFT regime		
m-Payments						
m-Money						

Example of Application in Jurisdiction "X"

	Inherent Risk Factors			*External Risk Factors*		
	Anonymity	**Elusiveness**	**Rapidity**	**Poor Oversight**		
m-fINFO	*0%*	*0%*	*0%*	*Low*		
m-BSA	*40%*	*40%*	*20%*	*Low*		
m-Payments	*50%*	*40%*	*10%*	*Medium*		
m-Money	*20%*	*50%*	*30%*	*High*		

Source: Authors' data 2008.

ML and TF Risks Inherent in the Four m-FS Service Categories

The following section presents the four service categories from most to least similar to traditional financial services. After defining each category, examples of the services are given along with their inherent AML and CFT risks. The inherent risks are discussed in conjunction with the external risk factors that can exacerbate them.

Mobile Financial Information Services (m-fINFO)

Definition and Examples. m-fINFO gives users the ability to view personal account data and general financial information without conducting transactions. m-fINFO is the most prevalent m-FS. It allows customers to view their account balance statements, transaction history records, exchange rates, stock quotes, receipts and confirmations for credit/debit card transactions, and credit limit alerts (see Figure 2). No financial transaction is initiated.

All of the visited jurisdictions offered m-fINFO, which served as the baseline for more advanced service delivery. It was observed that using mobile phones to access financial information saves time, minimizes fraud, and reduces opportunity cost of traveling to often remote financial institutions. See Table 7 in Appendix B for examples in each jurisdiction visited.

Identified Risks and Mitigation Measures. The use of mobile phones to access m-fINFO poses low risks from a ML and TF perspective because there are no transfer, deposit,

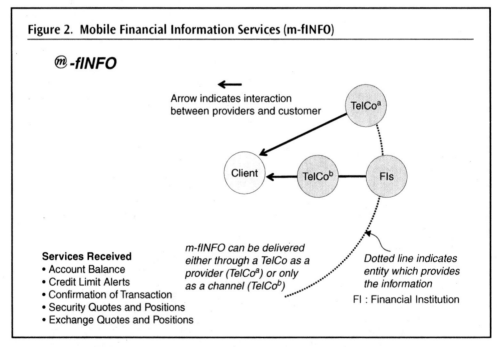

Figure 2. Mobile Financial Information Services (m-fINFO)

Source: Authors' fieldwork observations 2008.

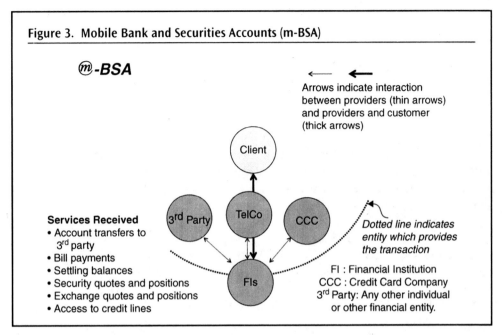

Figure 3. Mobile Bank and Securities Accounts (m-BSA)

ⓜ-BSA

Arrows indicate interaction
between providers (thin arrows)
and providers and customer
(thick arrows)

Client

Services Received
- Account transfers to
  3rd party
- Bill payments
- Settling balances
- Security quotes and positions
- Exchange quotes and positions
- Access to credit lines

3rd Party   TelCo   CCC

FIs

*Dotted line indicates
entity which provides
the transaction*

FI : Financial Institution
CCC : Credit Card Company
3rd Party: Any other individual
or other financial entity.

Source: Authors' fieldwork observations 2008.

withdrawal, or other options available. Providers and regulators, however, may need to address risks related to other issues like consumer protection, bank secrecy, and IT security.

The launch of m-fINFO services may signal that more services will soon be available. m-fINFO services are usually launched by providers to monitor the customer uptake of the service and to test the m-FS technology in a relatively safe environment. Once m-fINFO services are launched, regulators should anticipate that services may soon be expanded to include financial transaction capabilities.[36] Where this is the case, the role of the regulators and supervisors is to monitor the implementation of proper AML and CFT and risk management measures.

Mobile Bank and Securities Account Services (m-BSA)

Definition and Examples.   m-BSA allows bank and securities account holders to conduct transactions. The mobile phone is used to perform financial transactions similar to those conducted through other electronic banking channels such as ATMs, phone or Internet/ online banking (see Figure 3). It may also be used to trade securities from a customer's securities account. This service is widespread and has evolved from m-fINFO in response to customer need.[37] Examples of the service are person-to-person and person-to-business

---

36. Royal Bank of Scotland mobile phone service provides clients with an easy way to access account information (m-fINFO). It announced that m-BSA services will be added in the near future (Monilink 2007).

37. In many jurisdictions, this service is called "m-banking."

transfers, settlement of bill and credit card balances, foreign exchange operations, and stock and other securities' transactions.

Mobile phones as an electronic channel have the advantages of branchless banking and expansion of access to financial services to the poor (CGAP 2006). A mobile to mobile-phone remittance transfer service between Hong Kong SAR of China and the Philippines was launched in December 2006,[38] and was followed by a similar service between Malaysia and the Philippines in 2007. This new type of remittance transfer is currently being explored by other jurisdictions[39] because it reduces cost and covers remittance recipients who are unable to reach traditional banking distribution points.[40] In South Africa, mobile phones have enabled banks to expand financial service access to lower-income people who would otherwise not be able to acquire a bank account.[41] See Table 8 in appendix B for additional examples of m-BSA services.

Identified Risks. The primary ML and TF risks related to m-BSA are anonymity, elusiveness, and rapidity. m-BSA is the result of collaboration among various parties (banks, TelCos, and others), so transactions may be handled by different providers applying uneven levels of regulatory supervision. The services, however, are anchored in a bank or securities account under provisions that govern financial transactions and include supervisory controls.

m-BSA originates customer relationships without the customers' physical presence. Existing processes allow m-BSA providers to acquire new clients by opening accounts without the client's physical presence at a branch or, in some cases, without any face-to-face contact. Both off-branch and non-face-to-face procedures allow providers to reduce infrastructure costs associated with branch overhead and cost of customer acquisition.

The inability of the provider to recognize and verify customers' personal information signals a ML and TF anonymity risk. Customer anonymity may result from lack of instrumentation that allows customers to identify themselves. Or it could be the result of inadequate monitoring of who is actually conducting the transactions. Therefore, ML and TF risks may materialize during or after client acquisition.

Unauthorized users may obtain access to m-BSA and conduct illicit transactions. Money launderers may gain unauthorized access in the following ways: (i) when a mobile device is stolen and access to financial services is not otherwise protected with a security code, (ii) when a legitimate account holder passes on access to unauthorized users, and (iii) when a criminal breaches a provider's wireless network. In Brazil, for instance, poor people were targeted and paid by criminals to open bank accounts equipped with remote access channels (internet or mobile). After the accounts were opened, the authorized users would hand over their passwords to unauthorized criminal users.[42]

---

38. http://www.myglobe.com.ph/gcash/news.asp?articleid=2035.
39. For instance, by Safaricom in the UK-Kenya remittance corridor.
40. One of these services is also an example of m-Money.
41. Standard Bank of South Africa and MTN (a mobile service provider) have branded their jointly-owned m-BSA service as "MTN Banking." See http://www.mtn.co.za/?pid=242543.
42. In Brazil this practice affects standard bank-client business relationships and is referred to as "orange accounts." Combating this practice is a challenge for law enforcement.

Mitigation Measures.   Seven measures to mitigate ML risk for m-BSA services were identified in the jurisdictions visited. The mitigation measures focused on innovative Know-Your-Customer (KYC) procedures[43] to protect clients during off-branch transactions and non-face-to-face acquisition processes. The measures included advanced identification mechanisms; limited-amount transactions based on customer profile; rule-setting to monitor and identify transaction channels; and adoption of internal controls. (See Appendix C for further description of mitigation measures.)

- Innovative KYC Procedures. In response to the need to acquire customers by off-branch or non-face-to-face procedures, jurisdictions have adopted alternative verification measures. The main procedures implemented are (i) legal exceptions to verifying customer's residential address during initiation of the banking relationship (so long as transactions do not exceed prescribed limits), (ii) alternative verification methods,[44] and (iii) restricted functionality.[45] Rather than via face-to-face contact, customer identification is established by cross-checking customer information with third party databases, such as a national tax or social insurance databases, or other reliable sources like a TelCo's database of active customers. TelCos register customers for m-BSA services and other m-FS using mobile phones and the Internet, but these customers are restricted to basic transactions until they have a face-to-face screening.
- Limited transaction amounts and imposed reporting thresholds are the most popular control measures adopted by regulators and the private sector. The lack of data available on m-FS means that transaction limits were rarely set as a result of risk-based analysis.[46] Instead, limits for m-BSA transactions were set arbitrarily at levels similar to those for other channels, such as ATMs or the Internet. In Korea, however, limits have been set based on statistical analysis of the number and magnitude of transactions (see Box 4).
- Two- or three-factor authentication mechanisms avoid unauthorized use of existing m-BSA. Compared to cash, which can be lost or stolen and used immediately, mobile phones offer safer means for managing finance. The security of the device itself combined with personal passwords provides two deterrents to protect against unauthorized m-FS users. Fieldwork also revealed use of more advanced measures like biometric authentication and electronic signature (e-signature) to complete financial transactions. Although these systems tend to be available on more advanced

---

43. KYC is a standardized practice emphasized in the FATF 40+9 Recommendations.

44. The Philippines is in progress of passing a regulation that will allow building a database of unique ID numbers for the population. In the meantime, however, it is possible for people to obtain IDs from a number of sources (municipal registry of residents, certificate issued by village leaders, social security certificate, driver's license, passport) and use a minimum of 2 of them to open a bank account.

45. "Restricted functionality" is the industry term for limiting the range of services a customer can access until full and proper CDD and KYC procedures are performed.

46. Another approach is a point-based KYC approach. This system presumes that the more KYC evidence a customer is able to provide (national ID, driver's license, passport, physical presence, etc.), the more the customer can be trusted so services are offered proportionally to identification provided.

Box 4: Risk-based Determination of Transaction Limits: The Case of Korea

Electronic funds transfer law and supervisory regulations have established limits on transactions conducted using m-BSA in the Republic of Korea. The limits are based on a statistical analysis of the volume, frequency, and other data gathered by the Financial Supervisory Services. Transaction amounts (in Korean Won) are grouped into three categories that fall under increasingly stringent security measures relative to the transaction amount. Financial institutions may also apply greater security controls based on the preference of the customer.

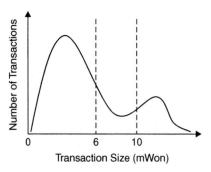

Category 1: W 0–6 million (US$ 6,000). Constitutes 85% of all transactions.

Category 2: W 6–10 million (US$ 10,000). Constitutes 5% of all transactions.

Category 3: W >10 million (>US$ 10,000). Constitutes 10% of all transactions.

Source: Authors' design from Korea Financial Supervisory Services (2007) data.

phones that are not affordable to low-income people, they are sometimes applied centrally by the service provider. A provider in South Africa, for instance, has tested a biometric voice identification system for m-FS.[47]

■ Customer profiling is a new tool being used to diminish the elusiveness risk. In several countries visited, banks have developed systems to monitor m-FS customer activities against their profiles by highlighting unusual transaction patterns. Profiles are built based on information provided at the time of customer acquisition and are modified on an ongoing basis. Data collected includes customer income level, transaction history, and services and channels frequently used. One advantage of customer profiling is that it does not require sophisticated software or complex IT rules (See Appendix C).

■ Identifying the channel used to conduct financial transactions is a key mitigation measure. Fieldwork revealed that in many cases, m-BSA providers were not able to identify the type of channel used for a given transaction.

■ Integrated internal controls effectively manage risks of real-time mobile transactions. The same technology that enables m-FS was also used by providers to moderate their exposure to risk. Unlike the use of manual controls only, which usually require time and recurring human intervention, banks, TelCos, and other m-BSA providers enhance manual controls with automated ones embedded in IT systems.

---

47. MTN Banking, a division of the Standard Bank of South Africa.

Table 2. Possible ML and TF Risks and Observed Control Measures for m-BSA

Type of Risk	Observed Risks	Mitigation Responses	Examples in Jurisdictions
Anonymity	Acquisition of customers off-branch or not in face-to-face meetings	Innovative KYC Procedures	**South Africa:** TelCo (Wizzit) representatives meet with clients in remote off-branch locations that are convenient for the customer **South Africa:** MTN-Standard Bank allows remote registration of new clients via Internet, call center, or mobile phone. Customer information is verified in 3rd party databases.
	Unauthorized use of m-BSA services through phone theft, passing a phone, or wireless on network breach	Advanced identification mechanisms	**Korea, Rep. of:** Electronic signature when using mobile phones for online services above certain value **Brazil:** HSBC confirms credit card transactions via mobile-phone text messages
Elusiveness	Using mobile phones at the layering stage of the ML process	Limits on transactions	**Korea, Rep. of:** Authorities determine limits on m-BSA transactions based on statistical evidence
		Customer profiling	**Brazil:** HSBC allows customers to individually set lower account limits than required by regulation **Korea, Rep. of:** As the amount transferred increases, banks are required to introduce more advanced security measures
		Monitoring	**Korea, Rep. of:** Banks have embedded a number of security rules into their IT systems that trigger a report to the FIU when met **Malaysia:** Maybank created a dedicated risk management team to address risks within the specific electronic channels
		Reporting	**Macao SAR of China:** An STR designed by the FIU contains a question indicating the channel of a suspicious transaction
Rapidity	Rapidity of m-FS transactions	Integrated system of internal controls	**Philippines:** TelCos enhance manual controls with automated ones embedded in IT systems

Source: Authors' fieldwork observations 2008.

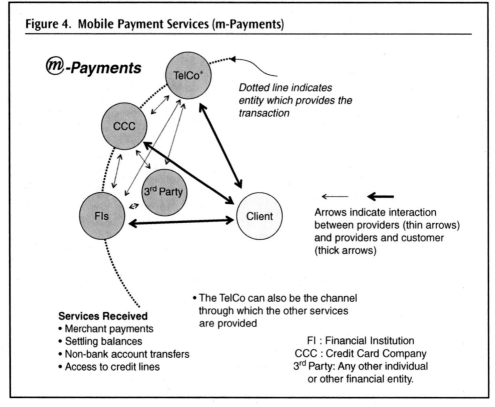

Figure 4. Mobile Payment Services (m-Payments)

Source: Authors' fieldwork observations 2008.

Mobile Payment Services (m-Payments)

Definition and Examples. m-Payments allow non-bank and securities account holders to make payments with mobile phones. Although transactions may eventually be processed by a bank in bulk, the fact that m-Payment services do not require an account with a traditional financial institution makes them distinct from m-BSA. The services are often carried out through a non-bank entity (such as a credit card company) and are not based on a pre-existing bank/securities account. As payment systems evolve with new technologies, m-Payments are likely to become popular because they do not face the same limitations as bank-anchored services or m-BSA. For example, a user's mobile phone can be used to make payments at a merchant's point of sale terminal (POS) or as a payment instrument similar to plastic (credit) cards. In some jurisdictions, as a precaution, accompanying security checks will continue to be sent to mobile users to confirm online transactions.

Identified Risks and Mitigation Responses. m-Payment services face the same risks and call for the same mitigation responses as m-BSA. The type of providers may vary, though, because their services are not grounded in a bank or securities account. Also, the services

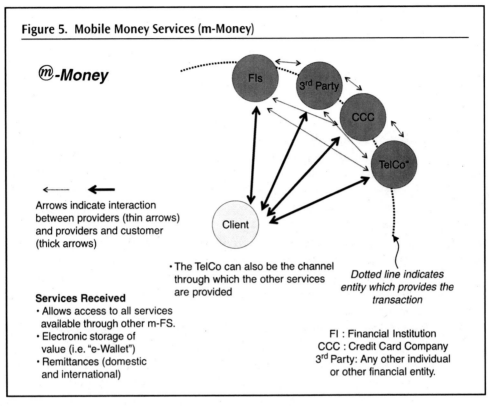

Figure 5. Mobile Money Services (m-Money)

Source: Authors' fieldwork observations 2008.

may be provided by non-traditional financial institutions with differing levels of control and supervision.

Mobile Money Services (m-Money)

Definition and Examples.   m-Money allows users to store value on their mobile phone or mobile phone account in the form of electronic currency that can be used for multiple purposes including transfers to other users and conversion to and from cash. One such example is the use of phone credits and airtime[48] as tender that users can trade for other goods and services. m-Money contributes to the development of mobile commerce and has an overall positive impact on the economy through increased velocity of money and swift settlement of transactions. Ultimately, it could also reduce the volume of cash in the economy.

---

48. In some countries, credit or airtime issued by a non-bank entity (often the TelCo itself) can be used as a form of currency. Users can transfer electronic currency to each other, use it to purchase items or redeem it for cash. One example is G-Cash in the Philippines.

m-Money is used in domestic and international remittances. In cross-border remittances, the study team observed TelCos facilitating transactions at both the origination and distribution sides, regardless of the settlement process.

Identified Risks. m-Money services create developmental opportunities, but also pose significant ML and TF risks. m-Money is the farthest-removed m-FS model from traditional financial services. It provides an entirely new way to conduct financial transactions and is the most rapidly developing m-FS category, so it carries the greatest potential for development as well as abuse. It poses all potential risks previously discussed[49] plus new risks identified in the team's fieldwork.

The elusiveness risk factor, observed in all m-FS categories, is particularly prevalent in m-Money. Appendix D provides a general overview of observed risks and mitigation responses for m-Money.

The use of multiple m-Money accounts facilitates untraceable transactions. Money launderers and terrorist financiers can make use of multiple m-Money accounts to hide the origin of funds. This method allows a large funds-transfer to be broken into smaller amounts, so the transfer appears less suspicious and is more difficult for providers and authorities to detect.

Cross-border remittances hold potential for terrorists and money launderers seeking to layer transactions. Taking advantage of the structural limitations on international law enforcement coordination and monitoring and detection systems, criminals may use cross-border remittances to render funds less traceable. The complexity of cross-border transfers can conceal the origin or destination of funds.

Mitigation Measures. A series of measures targeting consumers and retailers has been developed to reduce elusiveness. Consumer-oriented measures complement those developed for m-BSA services. Retailer-oriented measures are aimed primarily at protecting legitimate cross-border remittances from criminal interference. International m-Money transfers require enhanced KYC and due diligence requirements in some jurisdictions, and registration for cross-border m-Money providers was also required in some jurisdictions. Additional mitigation measures include limiting the number of accounts per customer, using a centralized registry of account holders (to prevent abuse of users with multiple m-Money accounts), and requiring authorization for retail points at which m-Money can be converted to physical cash.[50] In all cases, barring m-Money from being used in international remittances is an unfavorable response to diminishing the ML and TF risk. See Appendix D for a full description of these mitigation measures.

---

49. m-Money is the most versatile of all the services as transactions among subscribers of the same provider are settled outside the national payments system, which is overseen by regulator in most countries.

50. Some countries have prohibited the use of m-Money to thwart ML. In the most aggressive mitigation measures, jurisdictions have required that all person-to-person transfers go through the national payment system. This compels criminals to go through more regulated channels, but could have implications for efforts to expand access to financial services.

Observed Uses of m-FS.   Although m-FS services have been discussed individually in this paper for the sake of simplicity, the services can be, and often are, provided simultaneously.[51] Furthermore, in some instances one category is required for others to function. Some m-Money, m-Payment, and m-BSA services are built upon an earlier m-fINFO service. Where once only an account balance was shown, now a channel exists to conduct financial transactions on that balance. The examples illustrating the definition of each service (Figure 6 and Table 3) are not all-encompassing because m-FS is evolving rapidly.

ML and TF Risks External to m-FS Service Categories

Even though the risk is external, not inherent, to the services, poor oversight results in vulnerability for m-FS. The lack of coordination among authorities, exclusion from AML and CFT requirements, and the absence of fit and proper checks on m-FS providers hinder the ability of authorities to oversee m-FS. See Appendix D for further discussion of poor oversight.

Mitigation Responses

Collaboration among regulators was observed as the key measure to reduce the risks created by poor oversight in all jurisdictions visited. Financial sector regulators played a role in permitting m-FS providers to operate, even in non-traditional financial institutions such as TelCos.[52] In some jurisdictions the telecommunications regulator also played a role. Box 5 shows that financial and TelCo regulators leveraged their respective areas of expertise and agreed on the mutual areas of responsibility over bank and non-bank m-FS providers in Korea.

Policymakers and regulators in emerging m-FS markets engaged in an active discourse with the industry in order to maximize regulatory effectiveness, minimize costs, and ensure the full market was covered. In one jurisdiction, for example, operators are required to brief the Central Bank of any new m-FS at least thirty days prior to market launch.

Financial sector regulators in some jurisdictions issue licenses to m-FS providers to allow them to offer financial services. Licensing helps authorities scrutinize business models of prospective m-FS providers to ensure that the business is sound and proper. Registration allows authorities to know the service providers that are operating in the market.

Licensing requirements are used as a mitigation response in several jurisdictions. In South Africa and Brazil, for example, traditional financial service and m-FS providers need to be licensed as financial institutions. Such provisions have become one of the defining

---

51. Sometimes they are implemented gradually.
52. The key mitigation responses of licensing, supervision, and sanctioning were performed by the financial regulator.

Figure 6. Concurrent Use of m-FS

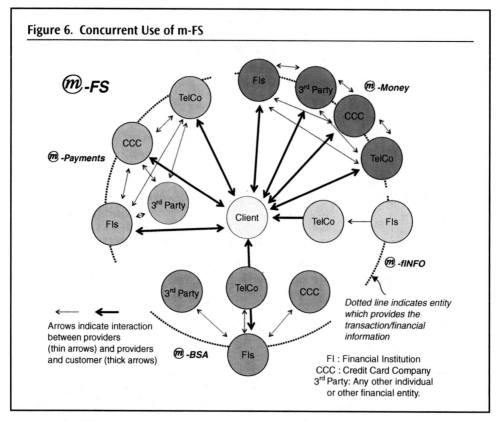

Source: Authors' fieldwork observations 2008.

Table 3. Concurrent Use of m-FS

Jurisdiction	m-fINFO	m-BSA	m-Payments	m-Money
Brazil	Banco Bradesco			
Brazil	Banco do Brasil			
Korea, Rep. of	Kookmin Bank			
Philippines	Globe			
Philippines	Smart			
South Africa	MTN - Standard Bank[a]			
South Africa	Wizzit-Bank of Athens			
Malaysia	Maxis			

Source: Authors' data 2008.
[a] m-Payment purchase of pre-paid electricity and airtime.

Box 5: Collaboration through Regulatory Dialogues

The Case of Korea: Financial and TelCo-Sector Regulators

TelCos in Korea developed "Phone Bill," an m-Payment service that allows subscribers to purchase goods and services online using their mobile phones and pay for them as part of their phone bill. TelCos seeking to add this service to their service profile approach their primary TelCo regulator within the Ministry of Information and Communication (MIC) to receive permission. MIC refers them to the Korea Financial Supervisory Services (FSS), the financial sector regulator, to obtain a license to provide m-FS. Although this coordination is not required under the law, it is considered good practice. It gives the TelCo regulator an opportunity to evaluate potential risks of new services and allows for closer collaboration between the TelCo and financial sector regulator.

The respective regulators have agreed on the scope of risks to be monitored by their agency, so MIC is largely monitoring IT risks, while Korea FSS handles other risks.

The Case of the Philippines: Regulators and m-FS Providers

The two leading Philippine m-FS providers have been in close communication with the Central Bank of the Philippines despite the fact that both providers, Smart Communications Inc. and Globe Telecom Inc., are non-bank institutions. Following an unprecedented level of dialogue, a number of actions were taken to better understand the business of the emerging m-FS players and its implications for the financial sector.

The institutional status of the m-FS providers was clarified in order to provide a legal foundation for the Central Bank and other public institutions to exercise their mandate. Globe was granted a license to operate as an RSP and entered a contractual arrangement with the Central Bank. Smart's m-FS business is subject to the Central Bank's supervisory scrutiny through Smart's bank partner, Banco de Oro. Supervisors may also conduct on-site inspections at Smart under a general provision allowing the supervisor to examine the outsourcees of banking services (in this case, the outsourcee of Banco de Oro). However, the same possibility to examine banks' outsourcees is not granted to banks' external auditors.

Both providers are subject to AML regulation. This includes the conduct of KYC procedures, record keeping and reporting of suspicious transactions to the Anti-Money Laundering Council. Reporting of STRs by both players is conducted electronically, and is required for all transactions above 500,000 pesos (~US$12,300). Over the last two years, Globe has submitted five STRs. Using special algorithms, the TelCos' systems detect fraudulent or terrorist financing patterns. These systems are even more robust than some of the systems utilized by Philippine banks. Under the contractual arrangement, Globe is also required to submit statistical reporting on their transactions.

Sources: Interviews at Bangko Sentral ng Pilipinas 2007, and Republic of Korea Ministry of Information and Communication 2007; [The Philippines] World Bank staff interviews 2007.

factors for partnerships between the TelCos and banks. This trend is clearly evident in South Africa in two business models: (i) Wizzit mobile operator and the Bank of Athens, and (ii) MTN mobile operator and Standard Bank. In the Philippines and Malaysia, non-bank providers are regulated by the financial sector oversight regulator and are licensed as either e-money issuers or RSPs.

Legal treatment of non-traditional m-FS varies from jurisdiction to jurisdiction. Table 4 illustrates the different types of licenses and requirements observed during fieldwork.

Table 4. Observed m-FS Licensing and AML and CFT Compliance Requirements

m-Financial Service	m-FS Provider	m-FS License Issued by FS regulator
m-fINFO	Bank, TelCo, any other entity	None
m-BSA	Bank, bank-TelCo partnership	Banking license
m-Payments	Bank, TelCo, credit card company, or other payment system provider	None [e.g. for Phone Bill in Korea, Rep. of, and Paggo in Brazil]
m-Money	Bank, TelCo, other entity	e-Money issuer RSP

Source: Authors' fieldwork observations 2008.

Box 6: IT Supervisory Core Group at a Central Bank

The Case of the Philippines

In November 2005, the central bank of the Philippines (Bangko Sentral ng Pilipinas) established a specialized team of former bank examiners and information systems experts, the Core Information Technology Support Group (CITSG) to keep pace with technological developments, better understand the potential risks of the emerging players, and supervise them effectively.

CITSG on-site inspections follow COSO[53] guidelines on internal controls, and among other aspects examine: logical access controls, record keeping, audit trail, disaster recovery and business continuity planning. This group studies m-FS and other electronic financial services, their risks, and effective supervision methods. All specialists are certified in information systems auditing.

Source: Interviews at Bangko Sentral ng Pilipinas 2007.

---

53. The Committee of Sponsoring Organizations of the Treadway Commission (COSO) developed a model for evaluating internal controls in 1992 that has been adopted as the generally accepted framework for internal control. It is widely recognized as the definitive standard against which organizations measure the effectiveness of their systems of internal control.

CHAPTER 4

Applying FATF Recommendations to m-FS

While the previous chapter addressed the observed and perceived risks of the m-FS categories, this chapter covers the extent to which the mitigation practices observed are actually consistent with the international AML and CFT standards. The second section of the chapter identifies the specific FATF recommendations that are relevant to m-FS. The third section addresses the application of AML and CFT standards to non-financial m-FS providers, particularly TelCos because they are the most predominant non-financial m-FS providers.

Observed Mitigation Responses and their Consistency with FATF Recommendations

m-FS providers are applying measures to reduce possible risks within all jurisdictions visited by the study team. Although the mitigation practices are motivated by commercial interests (managing fraud, credit, reputation, and other risk), they still reduce ML and TF abuse because m-FS providers have unintentionally laid the foundation for an AML and CFT regime.

This section classifies the different practices seen and discusses to what extent they meet the preventive requirements as set forth in the FATF 40+9 Recommendations (see Table 5). Drawing on the mitigation responses cited in Chapter 3, this section analyzes them by main areas of AML and CFT compliance:

- Licensing and registration processes
- Customer identification
- Record keeping
- Internal controls and monitoring

- Guidelines
- Reporting obligations
- Supervision and oversight
- Cross-border transactions
- Staff training

Licensing and Registration Processes

Licensing and registration processes are key to preventing criminals from controlling an m-FS provider and to ensuring the soundness of a company. There is a common consensus among stakeholders that m-FS need to be developed in a suitable regulatory environment that includes licensing or registration requirements. Although none of the visited jurisdictions issued specific regulations to m-FS providers, some did for specific m-FS activities (e-money issuance, remittance service provision). A regulatory framework—ideally based on type of services rendered—is needed to ensure that m-FS schemes are safe and m-FS providers are sound.

FATF standards address the risk that AML and CFT controls, which are assumed to be standard practice among traditional financial institutions, should also extend to cover TelCos. FATF Recommendation 23 stresses the need for jurisdictions to have proper licensing processes for financial institutions, which is consistent with the Basel Core Principles,[54] and is amplified by Special Recommendation VI (FATF 2003): "Each country should take measures to ensure that . . . legal entities, including agents, that provide a service for the transmission of money or value, including transmission through an informal money or value transfer system or network (mobile remittances) should be licensed or registered and subject to all the FATF Recommendations that apply to banks and non-bank financial institutions."

As a result, the licensing process is critical to ensure that m-FS providers can operate in a safe environment. Procedures to ensure that m-FS providers, mainly TelCos, are acting with proper authorization and are subject to prudent regulatory rules (AML and CFT) were observed in many of the jurisdictions visited.

In Malaysia, one of the main m-FS operators[55] is regulated not only as a TelCo and an e-Money issuer, but also as an RSP. Thus it is explicitly subject to the national AML and CFT law and to ongoing supervision by the Central Bank. Should a TelCo decide to provide e-money services in Korea, it would have to be licensed as a credit-specialized financial institution. In Macao SAR of China, a TelCo that provides financial services must be regulated by the Macao Monetary Authority (AMCM) and is subject to AML and CFT law.[56] In the Philippines, too, one of the main m-FS providers[57] was granted a license to

---

54. The Core Principles for Effective Banking, related methodology, updates, and proceedings can be found online at www.bis.org.

55. Maxis. Another m-FS provider is Mobile Money International.

56. Applicants should provide the regulator (DSRT) with their business plans. Also, all new projects developed after the license has been granted, changes in tariffs and promotions and new services (i.e. all that is outside the scope of the primary license) should be reported to the DSRT, which will look at the specifications and risk management procedures. This has been the case, for instance, when CTM engaged with Bank of China to launch the first mobile banking service in Macao.

57. G-Xchange.

operate as an RSP and therefore entered a contractual arrangement with the Central Bank (BSP 2007a, 2007b). In South Africa, for example, all m-FS providers must hold a banking license, and as such address the Central Bank's standards.[58] In Hong Kong SAR of China, mobile operators[59] are required to register as RSPs with the FIU and offer mobile remittance services.[60]

Customer Identification

Customer identification is key to building an effective AML and CFT regime. Customer due diligence (CDD) and KYC procedures are intended to enable a financial institution to form a reasonable belief that it knows the true identity of each customer and, with an appropriate degree of confidence, knows the types of business and transactions the customer is likely to undertake (FATF 2007). CDD and KYC principles are outlined in FATF Recommendation 5. According to the Recommendation, service providers that transfer money or value should take CDD measures by identifying the customer and verifying the customer's identity using reliable, independent source documents, data or information.[61] Moreover, Recommendation 5 underscores the need to conduct ongoing due diligence on the business relationship and scrutinize transactions undertaken throughout the course of that relationship to ensure that they are being conducted consistently. This means that the transactions should fit within the institution's knowledge of the customer's business and risk profile.

The risk of anonymity is aggravated when there is no face-to-face relationship between the customer and m-FS provider. Origination of customer relationship without the client being physically present increases the risk that m-FS providers will have insufficient data on a client.[62] FATF recommendations specifically address the ML and TF risks associated with new payment methods favoring anonymity like m-FS. As set forth in Recommendation 8 (FATF 2003), "Financial Institutions [banks and non-banks] should pay special attention to any money laundering threats that may arise from new or developing technologies that might favor anonymity, and take measures, if needed, to prevent their use in money laundering scheme." There are grounds to believe that Recommendation 8 also

---

58. These include: financial background and strength, governance, customer protection, safety and soundness of the system, background information on shareholders and managers; and business model. In practice, this requirement resulted in TelCo becoming in part a division of a financial institution, e.g.: MTN in Standard Bank and Wizzit in Bank of Athens.

59. Smartone Mobile Communications Ltd., CSL.

60. The HK FIU released a form (http://www.jfiu.gov.hk/eng/remittance.html#q01) where applicants need to identify themselves and provide a copy of their ID card/ Corporate/Business Registration Certificate, address and type of business, bank account to be used for business and contact information.

61. For legal persons, the implementation of Recommendation 5 requiring service providers and other financial institutions to take reasonable measures to understand the ownership and control structure of the customer is very theoretical since none of the visited TelCos offer m-FS to legal entities, but exclusively to individuals.

62. TelCos should not treat non-resident customers any differently than residents in terms of identification requirements. Many jurisdictions in which m-FS is predominant did not sufficiently perform CDD on non-residents. The study team recommends that TelCos perform enhanced KYC and CDD measures for such customers in the same way as banks take such measures.

applies to m-FS because the FATF refers explicitly to telephone banking as an example of non-face-to-face operations which, by nature, favor anonymity (FATF 2006a).

In light of the above, Recommendation 5 and Recommendation 8 mitigate the anonymity risk.[63] In m-BSA services, banks and securities firms are already implementing KYC diligences, regardless of the channel used to make transactions so the customer's identity is normally checked at the onset of the relationship. When it comes to a non-bank m-FS provider, as in m-Payment or m-Money, the risk of anonymity is normally addressed by applying FATF Recommendation 5 in the same way, which requires service providers to disallow anonymous accounts or accounts in obviously fictitious names. These service providers, like other financial institutions, should also undertake CDD measures, including verification of customer identity when establishing business relations.[64]

Several examples of risk mitigation practices in the jurisdictions visited reflect the Recommendations. In Korea,[65] for example, there are strict procedures to initiate m-FS and issue SIM cards. A customer needs to hold a bank account, come in person to a bank branch, provide identification,[66] and fill in a form (including details of predefined accounts to transfer money) to receive an e-banking ID and password. A letter is then issued by the bank so that the customer can obtain the SIM from the TelCo.[67] Service is available only to post-paid individual subscribers, not corporate clients, for whom the TelCo maintains full customer information.[68]

Further CDD practices to rule out anonymity are already in place. Customers using G-Cash[69] in the Philippines need to register via their mobile phones or the Internet. Following registration they may receive incoming m-Money transfers. However, they may not deposit or withdraw funds until undergoing face-to-face CDD, which can take place at a retail shop, an accredited business partner, or a partner bank.[70] In Hong Kong SAR of China, customers willing to use the mobile remittance service need to register their SIM card face-to-face with the mobile phone operators. Subscribers are required to present their national ID, which is equipped with security features and a chip with biometric information. In Macao SAR of China, the introduction of the new electronic national ID[71] has

---

63. All FATF recommendations mentioned in this section should be read in conjunction with the Glossary of the FATF (2006a), which gives a broad definition of Financials Institutions which encompass service providers that transfer money or value, and also electronic money providers.

64. This is not always the case when it comes to pre-paid cards.

65. In Korea, some banks have lately fallen victim to Internet and mobile phone phishing (fraudulent attempts to acquire sensitive financial or personal information, such as credit card information or Social Security numbers, by impersonating a business representative or trustworthy person. Phishing attempts are usually initiated through e-mail, phone calls or Instant Messaging). In response, banks have been encouraged to open accounts to customers with plain access via bank branches, and initiate Internet and mobile financial channels only after the customer's credibility has been established after a monitoring period.

66. A foreign citizen is required to present a valid passport.

67. A copy of the letter is retained by the TelCo.

68. For billing purposes.

69. G-Cash is an m-FS system developed by TelCo Globe's subsidiary, G-Xchange.

70. The central bank of the Philippines (Bangko Sentral ng Pilipinas) issued Circular 562, which broadens the scope of identification documents permitted. This is aimed at ensuring that access to financial services is not impeded by ID requirements.

71. Before Macao introduced the chip-based ID, one of the main telecom companies, CTM, faced problems with fake IDs (2 to 3 cases per month).

strengthened the identification process. South Africa allows non-face-to-face customer acquisition but requires that the m-FS provider find other means to verify identity such as back-checking customer information with a third-party database.

Similarly, CDD practices to mitigate TF risks are in place. Although there was no evidence that m-FS has been abused by terrorist financiers in the Philippines, TF remains a concern for policymakers.[72] The CDD procedures apply to all financial transactions in the Philippines, not just m-FS. Apart from the pattern recognition algorithms embedded in the TelCos' devices, the systems also verify their customer database against the Office of Foreign Assets Control list.[73]

Record Keeping

One of the most important features of an AML and CFT regime is the obligation of financial institutions to keep records of customer transactions. This facilitates the reconstruction of individual transactions and provides evidence for prosecution of criminal activities if necessary. FATF Recommendation 10 requires financial institutions to maintain all necessary records on domestic and international transactions for at least five years following the completion of the transaction.

Evidence from fieldwork has shown that m-FS providers keep customer activity records. TelCos call these records Customer Detail Records. They contain data related to a mobile operator's system usage and include identification of each mobile call's originating and receiving phone, duration, and other information.[74] They do not, though, record the content of the call. Although TelCos keep these records for billing purposes, they have been used by authorities to track potential ML and TF transactions. In addition to the Customer Detail Records, m-FS providers may retain records specific to the transactions for consumers above these thresholds.

m-FS providers keep records similar to banks, payment-system providers, and RSPs. For example, one Malaysian m-FS provider[75] keeps records of transactions for active customers on an ongoing basis. Once the relationship is terminated, the information is archived for seven years. In Hong Kong SAR of China, AML regulations for RSPs require that records be kept on all transactions over HK$ 8,000. However, transactions below HK$ 8,000 are recorded in the systems of the mobile RSP.

Internal Controls and Monitoring

Promoting effective internal controls and monitoring systems is critical for regulators and the industry. Although some control and monitoring devices were created to detect fraud and misuse, they are also relevant to AML and CFT. Regulators and policymakers are tasked with ensuring that m-FS is safe from abuse in order to facilitate acceptance by the

---

72. This is particularly true because of military groups present in the remote areas of Mindanao. As of yet, however, there is no evidence that potential terrorist financing activities have been channeled using mobile phone banking.

73. See, for example, Specially Nationals and Blocked Persons published by the US Department of Treasury Office of Foreign Assets Control. http://www.treas.gov/offices/enforcement/ofac/

74. For example, the amount billed for each call.

75. Maxis.

general public. For the industry, robust internal surveillance mechanisms are critical to protecting their business and reputation, and to building confidence among customers. Likewise, FATF Recommendation 15 clearly requires financial institutions (banks and non-banks) to develop AML and CFT programs (FATF 2003). These programs should include, among others, internal policies, procedures, and controls, including appropriate compliance management arrangements and an audit function to test the system.

Secure internal monitoring systems have already been put in place by several m-FS providers. Evidence from the field has shown that the Korean experience with a non-bank service called Moneta Cash[76] demonstrates the need to have internal controls and oversight. Moneta Cash, a closed-settlement subscriber system, allowed transfers of funds among its subscribers, who rapidly expanded to 3 million. This service did not go through a bank, and insufficient internal controls aggravated by a superficial supervisory framework resulted in an IT security breach in 2004. Subscribers' sensitive information became accessible through the Internet and was used by unauthorized users for illicit transactions. Following this incident, Moneta Cash was discontinued (Kim 2006). This case raised discussion about the regulation of privately-owned settlement systems, the need for stringent sanctions, and the importance of high-quality IT systems for banks and other institutions to safeguard electronic customer records and transactions.

Following data leaks, e-finance regulations have become more risk-sensitive. Korea, after the Moneta Cash experience, introduced new e-regulations that recognized the inherent ML and TF risks related to m-FS.[77] Banks in Macao SAR of China do not permit m-FS transfers outside of the same bank or internationally. In addition, transfers require that the accounts are pre-registered with the bank and initiated by face-to-face contact with the customer. Regulators in the Philippines impose limits on the amount of m-FS transactions to limit ML risks.[78] Additionally, a Malaysian bank[79] has a specialized group dedicated to risk management in electronic products to complement the institutional risk management team. The group plays an active role in developing new products and monitors automated controls in particular channels for fraud and ML detection.

Guidelines

FATF Recommendation 25 requires competent authorities to establish guidelines that will assist financial institutions to implement and comply with their AML and CFT obligations. At a minimum, the guidelines should give assistance on issues covered under the relevant FATF Recommendations including: (i) a description of ML and TF techniques and methods and (ii) any additional methods that these institutions could take to ensure that their AML and CFT measures are effective (FATF 2006a).

Few of the jurisdictions visited had issued guidelines to specifically address ML and TF concerns. In Hong Kong SAR of China, the Hong Kong Monetary Authority issued supervisory guidelines that are applicable to electronic banking services and include inter alia,

---

76. Offered by SK Telekom.
77. According to the Korea Federation of Banks (KFB).
78. The authorized transfers are: of 40,000 Pesos per day, 100,000 Pesos per month and a maximum balance of 100,000 Pesos.
79. Maybank.

Box 7: Guidelines Designed by Financial Institutions

The Case of Rural Banks in the Philippines

Several banks in the Philippines adopted G-Cash to disburse employees' salaries, make deposits, withdrawals, transfers and provide mobile lending services for their customers, who generally live in the remote countryside.

The Association of Rural Banks in the Philippines worked closely with the Central Bank to obtain necessary clearance to launch services based on the m-BSA platform. As part of this process, the Association shared a compliance manual for rural banks with the Central Bank. This manual, designed by the financial institutions themselves, is a step-by-step guide for rural banks interested in offering m-FS products and lays out a framework for financial, organizational and technological risk management measures, including AML and CFT, and guidelines for adoption of m-FS.

Source: Microfinance Access to Banking Services Program 2007.

Internet banking services, and mobile banking services.[80] In Korea, the Financial Supervisory Service issued guidelines to banks that offer m-BSA services to address IT security and other internal control matters. In Macao SAR of China, the Monetary Authority of Macao is in the process of drafting guidelines on electronic financial services, including m-FS, to emphasize internal risk management practices that allows for service development of the Internet, ATM, phone banking, and m-FS in a safe environment.

Reporting Obligations

Reporting suspicious transactions or activities is critical to a country's ability to utilize financial information to combat ML and TF and other financial crimes. Countries' reporting regimes are laid out in national law, requiring institutions to file reports when the threshold of suspicion is reached. FATF Recommendation 13 stipulates that if a financial institution suspects or has reasonable grounds to suspect that funds are the proceeds of a criminal activity or are related to terrorist financing, it should be required to report the incident promptly to the country's FIU. This is particularly relevant to m-FS because most suspicious activities are identified *ex-post*.

Several cases emerged during field work in which m-FS providers, TelCos in particular, were reporting risks in the same fashion as other financial institutions. In Hong Kong SAR of China, TelCos are reporting entities under the AML and CFT regime. In Korea, m-FS providers are also subject to the regime as reporting institutions to the Korean FIU (KoFIU).[81] This is also the case in Macao SAR of China, where the form for STRs contains a heading in which the reporting entity indicates the channel used including m-FS. Likewise, in the Philippines, reporting of STRs by m-FS providers is conducted electronically, and is required for all transactions above 500,000 Pesos.[82]

---

80. Accessible at: http://www.info.gov.hk/hkma/eng/bank/spma/attach/TM-E-1.pdf.

81. At the time of the study team visit, a number of STRs involving the use of mobile phones had already been reported. See also Chapter 2.

82. This is equal to approximately US$ 12,200. For the last 2 years, G-Xchange has submitted five STRs. Under the contractual arrangement, Globe is also required to submit statistical reporting on their transactions.

Supervision and Oversight

Given that weaknesses in financial oversight can threaten financial stability both domestically and internationally, FATF Recommendation 23 and the Basel Core Principles call on jurisdictions to have an effective supervisory regime in place to oversee all types of risks, including ML and TF risks. FATF Recommendation 23 stresses the need for all providers of financial services to be subject to adequate regulation and supervision:[83] "at a minimum, businesses providing a service of money or value transfer (. . .) should be licensed or registered, and subject to effective systems for monitoring and ensuring compliance with national requirements to combat ML and TF." Although the Recommendation does not specifically mention m-FS, it can be inferred that m-FS providers should be monitored. This is especially true when non-bank m-FS providers like TelCos offer m-Payment or m-Money, because poor oversight constitutes a predominant risk. Some prime examples of jurisdictions addressing this risk are Hong Kong SAR of China, where the Hong Kong Monetary Authority has set up a specific department to supervise electronic financial services, and Korea, where the Financial Supervisory Service checks if banks are providing m-FS safely.

Cross-Border Transactions

Elusiveness in cross-border transactions is a risk for all m-FS business models.[84] As discussed in Chapter 3, criminals may attempt to open multiple m-Money accounts to make transactions less detectable. This risk is even greater in the case of cross-border mobile remittances that could allow criminals to use cross-border m-Money remittances to layer transactions and conduct anonymous transfers.

FATF recommendations seem to constitute an adequate preventive framework for cross-border mobile phone financial services and associated risks. For example, Special Recommendation VII on wire transfers specifies the information that should accompany domestic and cross-border wire transfers. Financial institutions, including money remitters, are required to include accurate and meaningful originator information (name, address, and account number) on fund transfers and related messages that are sent and the information should remain with the transfer or related message through the payment chain. Other jurisdictions have dealt with this differently. A relevant example was observed in Macao SAR of China, where transfers outside of the same bank are not permitted and international remittances are prohibited. Similarly, Korean commercial banks do not allow the mobile-phone funds transfers between domestic banks or with banks abroad. Mobile-to-mobile phone remittances are, however, permitted in the Hong Kong-Philippines, Malaysia-Philippines and Malaysia-Indonesia remittance corridors.

Staff Training

International standards require financial institutions to provide their employees with AML and CFT training that is appropriate and proportional to the risks. This is stated in FATF

---

83. See also FATF (2006a), Special Recommendations, Recommendation 23, essential criteria 23.6 and 23.7.

84. This problem does not apply to m-fINFO.

Table 5. Most Relevant FATF Recommendations for Risk-Based Consideration			
Risk Factor	**m-BSA**	**m-Payment**	**m-Money**
Anonymity	Rec. 5	Rec. 5	Rec. 5
	Rec. 8	Rec. 8	Rec. 8
Elusiveness	Rec. 10	Rec. 10	Rec. 10
	Rec. 13	Rec. 13	Rec. 13
	SR VII		SR VII
Rapidity	Rec. 15	Rec. 15	Rec. 15
Poor Oversight	Rec. 13	Rec. 13	Rec. 13
	Rec. 23	Rec. 23	Rec. 23
	Rec. 25	Rec. 25	Rec. 25
	SR VI	SR VI	SR VI

Source: Authors' analysis based on FATF 2004, 2006.

Recommendation 15, which requires financial institutions to establish ongoing employee training to ensure that employees are kept informed of new developments, including information on current methods, techniques and trends in ML and TF. In the Philippines for example, cashing-in or -out of funds from a mobile phone is conducted exclusively by licensed partners that must undergo AML and CFT training delivered directly by the Philippine FIU staff. Such training allows for a reasonable level of trust in the conduct of KYC procedures at the counter. In South Africa, agents of one m-FS provider[85] must be trained and certified for AML and CFT.

Application of AML and CFT Standards to All m-FS Providers

The Breakdown of AML and CFT Obligations

The breakdown of AML and CFT obligations among varying providers is ambiguous.

The role of service providers, such as banks, TelCos, and credit card companies, varies with each service model. In some cases like m-fINFO or m-BSA (see Chapter 3), banks are the major or sole m-FS providers, with TelCos playing a secondary role by offering customers a means to initiate financial transactions and thus communicate with a bank. In these schemes, mobile phones users are necessarily bank accounts holders so it can be inferred that AML and CFT obligations fall under the bank responsibility as the primary and unique m-FS provider.

The level to which non-traditional financial institutions should be subject to AML and CFT is unclear to many. The AML and CFT obligations of a given provider are especially difficult to know in customer relationships that are not anchored by a bank or securities account (such as when a TelCo alone provides m-Payment or m-Money). The line between

---

85. Wizzit-Bank of Athens, South Africa.

services offered by financial and telecommunication providers has become blurred in recent years (see Chapter 3). There is a resulting apprehension that some m-FS providers such as non-banks may fall outside the regulations to which other institutions providing financial services must adhere. This concern is echoed by some policymakers and regulators.

Fieldwork showed that TelCo AML and CFT obligations are applied unequally in the observed jurisdictions. The majority of TelCo m-FS representatives met by the study team perform some KYC and CDD measures. These measures have generally been conceived for commercial purposes rather than for AML and CFT. Although these initiatives are often relevant, none are designed specifically to address ML and TF concerns.

Reporting of suspicious transactions is not an obligation for TelCos that provide m-FS in most of the jurisdictions visited. Evidence from the discussions with local authorities and industry suggests that there is no consensus on how to implement AML and CFT international standards within the telecom industry. Indications are that AML obligations are viewed as too burdensome and, ultimately, impractical. Such obligations are perceived to require the adaptation of personal data collection systems and internal administrative practices that would result in operators losing some of their customers. Industry is resistant to such regulations, as many in industry feel that implementation of AML and CFT would kill their business.

m-FS Providers as FATF Financial Institutions

The authors hold the view that TelCos and other non-bank entities that provide m-FS should not be left out of the regulatory umbrella. The FATF 40+9 Recommendations contain no specific provisions[86] governing AML obligations for TelCos (as opposed to financial institutions or designated non financial businesses and professions [DNFBPs]). The FATF provides some clues by referring to "E-money"[87] (the category into which some m-FS models fall), but does not give full direction for their classification. Yet from a risk management perspective, it seems difficult to justify excluding TelCos from the AML and CFT radar screen, especially those which provide financial services on their own (m-Payment and m-Money providers). In order to bridge this gap, it is necessary to consider how to tie TelCos to the FATF standards and determine to what extent they are subject to the FATF. This will clear any ambiguity on their status.

The FATF has established two basic types of institutions subject to AML and CFT obligations, financial institutions and DNFBPs. For the purpose of the discussion, it is key to determine whether m-FS providers such as TelCos should fall under the category of financial institutions rather than designated non financial businesses and professions. The response does not appear clear and may differ depending on whether more emphasis is given to the type of service provided or to the provider itself. Placing TelCos under the DNFBP definition may appear more appropriate at first sight because most TelCos are not directly involved in financial services provision and are therefore non-financial by default.

---

86. However, the FATF definition of "financial institution" is a functional one, implying that TelCos providing financial services are implicitly subject to the 40+9 Recommendations.
87. The FATF does not define however what E-money means. See FATF (2006a), Annex 1.

Deeper analysis reveals that TelCos do not fit well into the definition of DNFBPs as outlined by the FATF.[88] Moreover, three of the identified business models out of four analyzed in this survey consist of a TelCo providing customers with a means to transfer money.[89] It is therefore more appropriate to refer to the type of services provided than the type of provider to classify TelCos.

In the light of the above, the authors come to the conclusion that TelCos providing m-FS should be considered as "financial institutions," as defined by the FATF.[90] According to the FATF, "financial institution" means, among other things,[91] any person or entity who provides its customers with transfer of money or values services, or issues and manages means of payment, *inter alia*, electronic money. This is essentially the case in several business models analyzed in this working paper, and it is also true in practice. Although there is no specific regulation for m-Payments and m-Money in most of the visited jurisdictions, m-FS providers are often regulated by the Exchange Control Act and Payment System Act. They may also be classified as banks, RSPs, or e-money issuers[92] depending on their activities and, as such, subject to relevant AML and CFT obligations.

Along the same lines, Member States within the European Union have classified Electronic Money Institutions (ELMIs) as a sub category of credit institutions. Electronic money[93] can be considered an electronic surrogate for coins and banknotes, stored on an electronic device and is generally intended for the purpose of effecting electronic payments of limited amounts.[94]

Scope of AML and CFT Obligations Applied to TelCos

FATF standards offer flexibility to determine the scope of AML and CFT obligations to be applied to TelCos.

TelCos that offer m-FS, especially m-Payments or m-Money should be classified in the financial institution category as defined by the FATF. These operators and others that

---

88. According to FATF (2006b), DNFBP means (a) Casinos, (b) Real estate agents, (c) Dealers in precious metal, (d) Dealers in precious stones, (e) Lawyers, notaries and other independent legal professionals and accountants, (f) Trust and Company service providers (acting as a formation agent of legal persons; providing a registered office; acting as a trustee, etc.).

89. m-BSA, m-Payment, and m-Money.

90. TelCos that do not provide m-FS probably would not qualify as either financial institutions or designated non-financial businesses and professions.

91. For a complete list, see FATF (2006a), Annex 1.

92. In Malaysia, for instance.

93. Electronic money is defined in the E-Money Directive as monetary value stored on a chip card (pre-paid card or "electronic purse") or on a computer memory (network or software money) and which is accepted as a means of payment by undertakings other than the issuer. See Commission Staff, *Working Document on the Review of the E-Money Directive,* 2006.

94. The European Commission issued a Memo (07/152) to the recently published Payment Systems Directive (2007/64/EC). The Directive builds upon other EU laws in the subject of regulating payment systems within and among countries of the EU. The Memo clarifies that TelCos are subject to the laws governing payment systems when the TelCo is acting alone as the intermediary (i.e. not m-BSA)."Put simply, where a telecom operator makes a payment on behalf of a payment service user to a third party, the payment transaction will fall within the scope of the Directive when operator acts solely as an intermediary making the payment."

sponsor m-FS transactions should be legally and explicitly subject to the FATF recommendations the same as any other money or value transfer provider. They will likewise be subject to the same preventive responsibilities. For m-Money and m-Payments, a TelCo can become the primary financial service provider, which would ensure that customers are identified, such transactions are monitored, the service agent is supervised, and in case of suspicion, the relevant authorities are properly informed.

AML and CFT obligations should not be applied uniformly, particularly in cases such as application to TelCos. A one-size-fits-all approach carries the danger of requiring all transaction-sponsoring m-FS providers to meet all recommendations, which is likely to lead to overlap of efforts and excessive costs, and hinder development of m-FS. This is especially true in m-BSA when a financial institution is already managing the customer account and performing AML and CFT measures. In this particular circumstance, the TelCo is an intermediary which provides consumers value-added services. The bank is the primary financial service provider and as such, has already performed KYC and CDD measures.[95] The TelCo has also identified the customer for the establishment of the telecom line, so subjecting TelCos to the same AML and CFT requirements as banks leads to replication. Since the risks of ML and TF vary based on service, a service-based approach seems particularly relevant to determining the AML and CFT obligations of a provider.

Fears of impeding development efforts by overly stringent AML and CFT requirements could be allayed by applying the FATF 40 + 9 Recommendations through a risk-based approach. The FATF Recommendations contain language that permits governments to adopt a risk-based approach to combating ML and TF. Competent authorities have the discretion to waive some or all requirements based on analysis of the risk exposure and governments can permit financial institutions (banks and non-banks) to use a risk-based approach in discharging certain AML and CFT obligations. As set forth in the FATF Recommendation 5 on CDD and KYC: "in certain circumstances, where there are low risks, countries may decide that financial institutions [banks and non banks] can apply reduced or simplified measures" (FATF 2003). Adopting a risk-based approach ensures that governments, regulators, financial institutions, and others are able to ensure that measures to mitigate ML and TF risks are commensurate to the risks identified.[96] It seems adequate for m-FS and would permit the implementation of AML and CFT obligations in the m-FS industry without being overly burdensome.

AML and CFT procedures for m-FS providers should be designed in proportion to assessed risks. It is the duty of policy makers and regulators to determine within the different m-FS providers the higher risk areas that should be subject to enhanced procedures.[97] Conversely, this implies also that in instances where risks are low, simplified or reduced controls may be applied.

The application of a risk-based approach allows TelCos and other m-FS providers to exercise reasonable business judgment with respect to their customers. A risk-based approach

---

95. Subject to modalities of specific business models.

96. As a consequence, resources can be allocated in the most efficient ways. The principle is that resources should be directed in accordance with priorities so that the greatest risks receive the highest attention. See FATF (2007).

97. This would include measures such as enhanced CDD checks and enhanced transaction monitoring.

should assist providers in effectively managing potential ML and TF risks. The approach will also allow policy makers and regulators to set the minimum requirements to apply to TelCos.[98]

By this means, TelCos would only be responsible for certain AML and CFT obligations based on the service provided and their role in providing it. If a TelCo is the primary sponsor of an m-Money or m-Payment service, it would then be responsible to the same level of AML and CFT safeguards as any other financial institution performing such transactions. In cases where the TelCo is working with an existing financial institution to deliver m-BSA services, the TelCo would be liable for *only* simplified CDD and *some* control measures while the other responsibilities would fall to the partnering financial institution. Defining which measures belong to each can be determined by assessing which is in the better position to do them.[99]

---

98. As set forth in FATF (2003), Recommendation 23, "other financial institutions should be licensed or registered and appropriately regulated, and subject to supervision or oversight for anti-money laundering purposes, having regard to the risk of money laundering or terrorist financing in that sector. At a minimum, businesses providing a service of money or value transfer, or of money or currency changing should be licensed or registered, and subject to effective systems for monitoring and ensuring compliance with national requirements to combat ML and TF."

99. In the m-BSA model, for example, a bank manages the account so it is in a much better position to perform most if not all the AML and CFT requirements. In some cases and for some requirements, the TelCo may be in a better place than the bank, for example in South Africa, the TelCo (Wizzit) performs the initial CDD measures while the bank (Bank of Athens) monitors the transactions, does ongoing CDD, and other AML and CFT requirements.

CHAPTER 5

Conclusions and Policy Recommendations

This section presents conclusions from the field work and research conducted by the study team. It also reflects internal discussions on the development of new technologies and, specifically, the use of mobile phones for financial services. The chapter concludes with recommendations to key stakeholders in implementing mobile phone financial services in a safe and sound environment.

Conclusions

The observed ML and TF vulnerabilities of m-FS do not justify the risk perceptions discussed in Chapter 2.[100] The risks do not appear any higher than those for other channels to access financial services.[101] In fact, m-FS can offer a greater level of security. In most of the jurisdictions visited, transactions are easily traceable and are limited by amount, nature, and frequency. Furthermore, the fact that most providers offer limited cross-border functionalities and Customer Detail Record (CDR) protocols ensures that detailed record keeping

---

100. These risk perceptions explained in Chapter 2 are: unknown identity, false identification, pooling and delegation, smurfing, speed, and m-FS providers falling outside the regulations.

101. At present, many of the security features of e-money schemes, including the limits on the value that can be stored on cards, make them less attractive for the purposes of money laundering and other criminal abuses. For many observers indeed, in view of the low average amounts involved in m-FS and electronic money broadly speaking, full application of identification and record keeping requirements could render such systems uneconomic. See also the *Working Document on the Review of the E-Money Directive,* available at http://ec.europa.eu/internal_market/bank/e-money/index_en.htm.

and monitoring processes are in place.[102] In the m-BSA service type, for example, it is quite possible that KYC procedures are done twice for the same consumer, both by the bank holding the financial account and the TelCo managing the connection.

The international standards set by the FATF address the vulnerabilities of m-FS. As demonstrated in Chapter 4, all observed ML and TF risks associated with m-FS are mitigated by the proper implementation of the FATF 40+9 Recommendations. There seems to be no need at present to create new or adjust the existing recommendations to cover m-FS.

Policymakers face the challenge of effectively implementing FATF standards while enabling the development of m-FS. Full effectiveness can be achieved by taking advantage of the flexibility granted by the international standards and a risk-based approach. Although this paper is not aimed to assess compliance with the standards, the findings show that some jurisdictions are not fully leveraging this flexibility.

A poor or non-existent AML and CFT regime could undermine sustainable development of m-FS. AML and CFT requirements should not be perceived as an impediment for m-FS development, but rather as an opportunity to ensure that development of m-FS is growing in a safe and sound environment. Jurisdictions may wish to consider the policy recommendations that follow.

Fieldwork has shown that most m-FS providers apply risk mitigation measures that are compatible with AML and CFT obligations even if they were not conceived to combat ML and TF. This supports the view that the implementation of AML and CFT measures is not an obstacle to business growth. In countries where m-FS is less developed or is growing slowly, discussions with the authorities revealed that market saturation or easy access to finance through other channels were the primary hindrances to m-FS development.

A service-based approach is preferable to a provider-based one for determining the actual level of ML and TF risk. As outlined in Chapters 3 and 4, such an approach aids policymakers and regulators in targeting mitigation measures to the actual level of risk. A service-based approach is also risk-based because risk varies by the service and not the provider, as business models of providers vary by jurisdiction.

Policy Recommendations and Issues for Consideration

Policymakers

1. m-FS offers an opportunity to improve access to finance and should be developed as such. Policymakers should engage in a policy dialogue with stakeholders to develop an enabling environment for new technologies. Given the potential that mobile phones offer in developing economies, the convergence financial and non-financial services should be encouraged. m-FS should not be perceived as an end-all solution though, but as a component of a broader strategy for financial inclusion.

---

102. According to FATF (2006b): "mobile payment programs that draw on a prepaid account can be funded in a variety of ways. Payment sources that have independently verified the identity of the phone owner and that maintain a record of the funds transfer to the mobile payment account present a low risk. The use of cash to fund a mobile payment account, independent of other risk factors or risks mitigation strategies, may present some limited ML and TF risks" (19).

2. An effective AML and CFT regime enhances market integrity and, therefore, the sustainability of the m-FS business models. Private sector entrepreneurs require certainty for reducing their exposure to risks such as ML. They are also averse to reputational risks associated with TF.

3. m-FS providers that give access to financial transactions should be clearly identified as being subject to AML and CFT laws. Although many m-FS providers are already operating their business in a way that is consistent with AML and CFT,[103] they are not explicitly mentioned in observed legal structures as having specific AML and CFT responsibilities. Unequivocal legal obligations would ensure there are no gaps in the regulatory umbrella and provide a level playing field for all providers in the m-FS market.

4. Risk assessments should be conducted prior to legislating controls because mitigation measures vary by jurisdiction. As noted in Chapter 3, business models and risks vary from jurisdiction to jurisdiction. A risk-based approach offers great flexibility in the application of mitigation measures. The level of risk greatly depends on the nature of the particular services provided so the necessary level of controls will fluctuate. This requires gathering statistics to allow national stakeholders to (i) better understand the issues, (ii) gauge the magnitude of risks, and (iii) take the appropriate policy measures.

5. Policymakers should consider measures to strengthen and standardize the national public identification systems to improve m-FS providers' ability to perform CDD. As observed in the fieldwork and noted by recent research (Bester and others, Forthcoming), instruments for customer identification are a key component for an effective AML and CFT regime. Regardless of provider-type,[104] all m-FS models have processes for identifying customers. Such processes are present even though the reasons for requiring IDs are not necessarily related to AML and CFT compliance. This implies that the need to determine the identity of the customer relies heavily on the public identification system that a jurisdiction has. This is particularly relevant to m-FS among other channels as its reach can go well into rural and poor communities where national identification systems may be weak.

6. Policymakers should consider the inclusion of alternative instruments to comply with ID requirements. It is inadequate for an AML and CFT regime to require m-FS providers to comply with CDD measures without producing a reliable means to do so. IDs cannot be linked to extensive verification procedures that increase the cost of compliance as a surrogate activity that belongs to the State. If the public infrastructure for IDs is not sufficiently secure, policy makers face the challenge of identifying which IDs could complement or substitute public IDs.[105]

7. Business models in which there is more than one financial service provider should be analyzed on a risk basis so that AML and CFT requirements are met and that there is no

---

103. It is clear that many AML and CFT requirements, such as knowing clients, can be a tool for business development. This would also apply to other areas of good business practice such as safety for debt collection, consumer protection and collaboration with law enforcement authorities to mitigate commercial and reputational risks.

104. Whether a bank, TelCo, or other m-FS provider.

105. On the origination of remittance transfers in Hong Kong SAR of China, authorities have allowed money transfer operators to process transfers to those that are able to provide a valid ID.

redundancy in implementation. Responsibilities of risk mitigation should fall proportionally to a provider's participation in the transaction. In collaborative business models in which both a bank and a TelCo take part in providing the financial service, it is important that clear lines of responsibility are drawn between the two players. This will ensure that there are neither redundancies nor gaps in AML and CFT controls.

8. Non-face-to-face customer acquisition is encouraged as long as effective alternatives mitigate the anonymity risk. Non-face-to-face customer acquisitions were identified as one of the greatest vulnerabilities of offering financial services through mobile phones.[106] The prohibition of non-face-to-face customer acquisition is one of the greatest impediments to expanding financial access. In many cases, alternatives exist through new technologies and processes to diminish these risks.

In markets where this is especially relevant and the use of such technology does not hinder the poor from access m-FS, guidelines should be distributed to m-FS providers that detail the use of new technological solutions for facilitating non-face-to-face customer acquisition. In order to create such guidelines, new solutions should be tested by regulators and implemented gradually until there is a level of comfort on security of procedures and reporting of suspicious transactions.

9. Policymakers should take advantage of the full flexibility permitted by the AML and CFT international standards. The FATF 40 + 9 Recommendations were crafted in such a way that their implementation should not be an impediment to business development. This full flexibility has not always been utilized, which could slow market growth.

FIUs and Law Enforcement

1. Financial intelligence and law enforcement authorities should develop clear rules and guidelines for m-FS transaction providers. Although TelCos already require information from their customers for business purposes, the team observed that uniform standards do not exist on the type and extent of information m-FS transaction providers[107] should request. Lack of guidance is all the more onerous due to the temptation for TelCos to protect themselves from liability by gathering excess information that is ultimately useless for AML and CFT and may hinder economic development.

2. Authorities should ensure they have the capacity to analyze information reported by TelCos that provide m-FS. In some developing countries law enforcement and criminal judges do not have the technical or professional capacity to analyze information stored by TelCos.[108] To detect criminal or TF activity, it is imperative that such information be made available to and fully processed by intelligence and law enforcement authorities.

---

106. This was also cited in other new financial services such as Internet banking. See Bester and others (forthcoming).

107. It is important here to note that m-FS transaction providers do not include m-fINFO services which were not observed to carry any ML and TF risk because they do not allow for financial transactions, only information services.

108. For example, in some jurisdictions the computer systems of the TelCos were far more advanced than that of the FIU or banks, meaning that the FIU was not able to analyze m-FS data to the same level it was for banks.

3. STRs would be more effective if they always include data on the type of channel used. The authors view this as a critical step for law enforcement and FIUs to detect criminal activity and will help authorities to conduct typology research and learn how to disrupt and prevent such illicit transactions.

Sector Regulators

1. The convergence of financial and mobile communications industries requires greater collaboration among sector regulators. In order to best enhance AML and CFT regimes and prevent over-regulation, TelCo and financial regulators must coordinate with each other to ensure the regulatory umbrella does not have gaps and is not redundant.

2. Regulators should note that m-fINFO is likely to be an early sign that more sophisticated and potentially riskier mobile services are ahead. It has been the case in many countries that m-FS were first introduced as information-based services that did not allow transactions. After a time, m-fINFO was often supplemented with transaction-enabling services (such as m-BSA, m-Payments, and m-Money) that carry greater ML and TF risks[109] and therefore require more financial sector supervision.

3. Licensing/registration and ongoing monitoring of m-FS providers should be implemented. As observed during fieldwork and recommended by the FATF, licensing for financial service providers is an effective way to make certain m-FS providers adhere to AML and CFT procedures and prevent potentially hazardous business models from reaching the market. Such practices can be useful to mitigate risks by helping regulators stay aware of important changes in the market.[110]

In addition to verifying that a business model is sound, licensing may also prevent criminals and terrorist financiers from creating shell corporations through an m-FS platform.[111] Regulators should consider making fit and proper requirements similar to those already in place for banks and other financial institutions. Fit and proper requirements are consistent with the fiduciary obligations of good business practices and not solely for AML and CFT purposes.

4. Transaction limits are critical to mitigating risks. The authors strongly support the notion of transaction limits to be set in consultation with m-FS providers. Such limits should be made so as to balance business needs with safety requirements.

Supervisors

1. The potential risks associated with m-FS should be given the same level of attention as those linked to other financial channels. Competent supervisors should include relevant

---

109. Transaction-enabling services hold greater risks than m-fINFO because they allow for the transfer of money, a key part of the laundering of money.

110. If one business model, m-fINFO for example, is being replaced by a potentially riskier one (m-BSA, m-Payments, m-Money).

111. Shell corporations are front companies that are used to hide funds and clandestinely funnel money for criminal purposes.

m-FS risks into the scope of their onsite and offsite duties so as to avoid holes in the implementation of AML and CFT regulations.

2. Examiners should be well-trained and given access to each business. In order to assess the true level of AML and CFT compliance, examiners should be sufficiently trained and have access to business records with specific instances of transactions being performed over a mobile phone. They should also be able to view how certain internal rules are made. For instance, supervisors should be able to know who defines the transaction limits and why.

3. Information technology of m-FS businesses should become an integral part of supervision. It is recommended that supervisors be able to monitor the growth of new technologies in a business. This means that technological monitoring systems and inspections in addition to IT training may be crucial in some instances where IT is central to the delivery of a financial service.

Bank m-FS Providers

1. Collaboration with regulatory institutions in the development of AML and CFT controls will aid in sustainable market creation for m-FS. Authorities will better understand the market and be more able to appropriately target controls. Applying controls on a targeted basis and with the input of business will help form a vibrant, enabling environment for businesses to develop.

2. m-FS should be included as a distinctive channel in the scope of banks' AML and CFT monitoring to contribute to its overall risk assessment. Banks should expand their AML and CFT controls to cover m-FS. Initial and ongoing screening of ML and TF risks should recognize the distinctiveness of the m-FS channel and help design controls commensurate to its specific vulnerabilities. This will better enable the bank to prevent abuse.

3. Banks should enhance CDD and KYC training tailored to m-FS for staff and utilize IT systems. Banks should develop training that is tailored to the specific characteristics of m-FS. For instance, training should expand from front office to back office functions because m-FS is more likely to be encountered by those in the back office. In addition, banks should take advantage of information technology systems to prevent abuse of m-FS.

Non-Bank m-FS Providers

1. Non-bank m-FS providers should collaborate with authorities to launch and sustain m-FS. When authorities understand business models, they can develop appropriate regulations that may result in limited or reduced compliance costs. m-FS providers should approach authorities with their business plans to launch new services early, so as to ensure that the regulator will set an enabling environment that recognizes the value added to businesses and consumers. Otherwise, authorities will shape the regulatory response by unwarranted risk perceptions.

2. TelCos should not treat non-resident customers any differently than residents in terms of identification requirements. Many jurisdictions in which m-FS is predominant did not sufficiently perform CDD on non-residents. The study team recommends that TelCos perform enhanced KYC and CDD measures for such customers in the same way that banks take such measures.

Self-Regulating TelCo Industry Organizations

1. Self-regulatory organizations should work with foreign counterparts to perform AML and CFT analysis. Self-regulatory bodies can be used to improve AML and CFT compliance in m-FS. As authorities work hard to catch up with the industry in terms of appropriate legislation, self-regulatory organizations can work with their foreign equivalents to determine best practices for the industry and how to improve each.

2. Self-regulatory organizations should raise awareness within their industry. It was observed that many TelCos felt they were not responsible for AML and CFT since they were technically not part of the financial industry. The self-regulatory organization should work to make industry members more aware of the potential risks associated with m-FS and their obligations under the law.

The Financial Action Task Force (FATF)

The following paragraphs are intended to supplement the work that has been done by the FATF in regard to ML, TF, and new technologies.

1. The FATF may wish to consider treating TelCos that facilitate transactions as financial institutions. FATF 40+9 Recommendations sufficiently cover the risks associated with m-FS. However, as TelCos' primary business is communication not finance, ambiguity remains (especially within the industry) as to whether they should be subject to the FATF recommendations prescribed for financial institutions. The study team feels the industry and regulators would benefit from a clear recognition of financial institution status for TelCos that provide financial transactions.

2. After this, assessors should consider m-FS when applying the FATF methodology to country AML and CFT compliance. As m-FS grows in popularity, the significance of this channel on money flows is becoming increasingly relevant. It is critical that assessors[112] take m-FS into account when performing AML and CFT compliance assessments. Also, because risks and their proper controls vary by service category and not provider-type, it is suggested that assessors make use of the categories outlined in Chapter 3 to evaluate compliance.

---

112. Assessors here refers to those from the FATF, FATF-styled regional bodies, World Bank, and IMF.

m-FS Growth

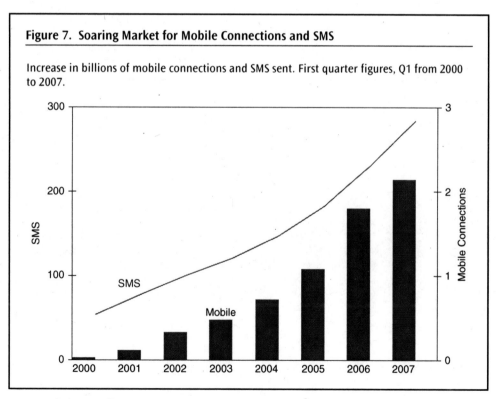

Figure 7. Soaring Market for Mobile Connections and SMS

Increase in billions of mobile connections and SMS sent. First quarter figures, Q1 from 2000 to 2007.

Source: Wireless Intelligence 2007.
Note: First quarter data.

Table 6. Factors Contributing to Growth of m-FS

Factor	Description
Very Low Infrastructure Requirements	m-FS can be added to existing mobile technologies. Unlike Internet-banking, which requires infrastructural investments in computers and broadband, m-FS can be expanded quickly for relatively little expense.
Low Costs and Increased Convenience	As opposed to traditional financial services, costs borne by the financial institution and passed on to the consumer are small. Additionally, as the service does not require physical access to a financial institution, it allows access to those residing too far from bricks-and-mortar financial service providers.
Small Transactions	High minimum-transaction amounts excluded many people from traditional financial services. Many services that offer fund-transfers require a minimum transaction amount or minimum account balance. m-FS allows small sums to be transferred.
Cross-border Remittances	Migrant workers typically use traditional or informal remittance systems to send money to their home country. Their transactions are frequent, often small in amounts, with both senders and receivers being highly conscious of associated fees. m-FS offers a competitive advantage over wire transfers and traditional finance channels.
Security Features	m-FS could potentially automate transactions that are done manually on paper in many jurisdictions. Electronic transactions can be automatically stored and quickly traced, and m-FS offers additional methods to verify user identity when conducting transactions. Password protection and other personal identification systems are two such options.

Source: Authors' data 2008.

Types of m-FS and m-FS Services Observed in Fieldwork

Table 7. m-fINFO in Visited Jurisdictions

Jurisdiction	Service Provider	Services Offered
Brazil	Banco Itau	Text message to confirm a credit or debit card transaction (including those not originating via m-FS)
Brazil	Banco Bradesco	Text message to confirm a credit or debit card transaction
Brazil	Caixa Econômica	Balance inquiry and one-time passwords for Internet transactions
Korea, Rep. of	Kookmin Bank	Balance Inquiry
Korea, Rep. of	Kium/Daewoo/Samsung	Stock Quotes
South Africa	Standard Bank	Balance Inquiry
Philippines	Asia United Bank	Balance Inquiry
Malaysia	Maybank	Balance Inquiry

Source: Authors' data 2008.

Table 8. m-BSA in Visited Jurisdictions

Jurisdiction	Service Provider	Services Offered
Brazil	Banco Itau Banco Bradesco	Transfer funds between accounts
Hong Kong SAR of China	DBS Bank	Transfer funds between accounts and trade on the stock exchange
Korea, Rep. Of	Kookmin Bank	Transfer funds between accounts
Korea, Rep. of	Kium/Daewoo/Samsung	Trading stocks
Macao SAR of China	Bank of China, BNU	Transfer funds between accounts, bill payment, and settlement of credit card balances
Malaysia	Maybank	Transfer funds between accounts
Philippines	Bank of the Philippine Islands	Disbursement of loans, payroll services, and loan repayments
South Africa	MTN and Standard Bank	Transfer funds between accounts
South Africa	ABSA Bank	Distribution of pensions using a service called "ALLPAY"

Source: Authors' fieldwork observations.

Table 9. m-Payments in Visited Jurisdictions

Jurisdiction	Service Provider	Services Offered
Brazil	Paggo	Payment services through mobile phones to customers without a bank account
Korea, Rep. of	All TelCos in Korea	Taxi drivers use mobile phones as a terminal for customers to pay fares

Source: Authors' fieldwork observations.

Table 10. m-Money in Visited Jurisdictions

Jurisdiction	Service Provider	Services Offered
Philippines	Smart Communications, G-Xchange	▪ E-money transfers between subscribers ▪ Refill e-money accounts with bank wire transfers ▪ Receive international remittances ▪ Receive payroll ▪ Make payments ▪ Loan disbursements and repayments ▪ Purchase airtime
Malaysia	Maxis, Mobile Money International	▪ E-money transfers between subscribers ▪ Refill e-money accounts with bank wire transfers ▪ Receive payroll ▪ Receive and send international remittances ▪ Make payments ▪ Loan disbursements and repayments ▪ Purchase airtime ▪ Near-Field Communication POS transactions

Source: Authors' fieldwork observations 2008.

Mitigation Measures for m-BSA

This Appendix expands on earlier discussion on mitigation responses observed in m-BSA practices. It further examines the following points:

- Mitigation of anonymity for acquisition of customers by off-branch or non-face-to-face procedures
- Mitigation of unauthorized use of an existing m-BSA
- Mitigation by limiting transaction amounts and imposing reporting thresholds
- Mitigation using customer profiling
- Mitigating the elusiveness by using rules for monitoring
- Mitigation through integrated internal controls

Mitigation of Anonymity for Acquisition of Customers by Off-branch or Non-face-to-face Procedures

Transaction limits and alternative verification methods are useful mitigation responses. In South Africa, under a legal exception in that country, banks are not required to verify the residential address during initiation of relationship with a customer so long as transactions do not exceed prescribed limits. This provision allows for customer origination to take place in an off-branch and non-face-to-face environment and has been introduced by an m-BSA provider.

Cross-checking with third party databases is the observed mitigation response for non-face-to-face transactions. Providers in visited jurisdictions are required to employ KYC procedures for new customers, regardless of whether the account is opened using a mobile phone, an interactive voice response system, or the Internet. In face-to-face practices, the customer is

---

Box 8: Non-face-to-face Risk Mitigation Responses: The Case of South Africa

Terms under which non-face-to-face customer acquisition are permitted:

FIC Exemption 17 (2001)

- Maximum balance R25,000 ($3,570)
- Maximum transaction value R 5,000 ($714) per day or R25,000 per month
- No international transactions (other than cash withdrawals in Common Monetary Area)
- One such account per person
- Account may only be held by a South African citizen or resident

Banks Act Circular 6

- Non-face-to-face processes must be limited to Rand$1,000(USD$145.9) per day.
- the bank must search for equally secure substitute methods to identify the client (such as matching the ID number to a range of independent credible data bases and monitoring the movements on the account)

Source: Hoffman 2007; South African Financial Intelligence Center 2004; South African Reserve Bank 2006; World Bank staff interviews 2007.
* Currency conversion on Bloomberg, Oct 17, 2007.

screened visually (and copies of original IDs are taken). Alternatives means are allowed to verify the information provided by the customer. Such information may be verified by the provider against a national database of identification (tax or social insurance databases).

Third party databases with information gathered on post-paid subscribers, like TelCo billing records, is used for anti-fraud purposes. However in some countries, customer records are even required for pre-paid accounts.[113] After such information is cross-checked by the m-FS service provider, there is no need for additional verification.

Mitigation of Unauthorized Use of An Existing m-BSA

Biometric authentication systems were observed as new mitigation measures in some jurisdictions. ID cards equipped with a memory chip include personal information (biometric authentication systems) to be used to authenticate the user. For example, banks and TelCos in Macao SAR of China were facing problems with fake IDs (reporting two to three cases per month) before the introduction of the ID cards equipped with a chip. Since then, the reported use of fake IDs has ceased. In Korea, another security measure that has been widely adopted is the use of an electronic signature for financial transactions.[114] Currently, about 17 million people use them.

---

113. A few countries engaged in "registration," by requiring operators to register the identity of all mobile phone subscribers, including pre-paid subscribers.

114. An electronic sound, symbol, or process, attached to or logically associated with a record and executed or adopted by a person with the intent to sign the record. 1999 Uniform Electronic Transactions Act released by National Conference of Commissioners on Uniform State Laws NCCUSL.

Box 9: Customer Profiling Systems for AML and CFT

The Cases of Macao SAR of China and Hong Kong SAR of China

Bank of China (Macao SAR of China) operates a centralized system to detect suspicious trans-actions that includes mobile and other types of transactions. The system monitors transactions and generates reports on an ongoing basis. It checks if transfer limits were observed and if the number of transactions is within limits. Then it verifies consistency between clients' income levels and the types of services used. The system assigns different risk weights to different clients. The clients' risk grade reflects, on a scale of 1 to 6, information about individual pro-files, occupations, sources of funds, country of residence/business and type of transactions usu-ally conducted.

Similarly, an internal monitoring system at HSBC (Hong Kong SAR of China) allows the bank to iden-tify a transaction that deviates from the customer's typical profile. It also matches it against a group of customers who share the same profile. Although unusual patterns of behavior matter most in determining risk, the Bank can also assign higher or lower risk ratings for specific deliv-ery channels. For instance, customer transactions conducted through the Internet or an ATM may be considered more risky than those conducted through a mobile phone, or vice versa.

Source: World Bank staff interviews 2007.

Mitigation by Limiting Transaction Amounts and Imposing Reporting Thresholds

Setting limits was observed to be the most popular control measure adopted by regulators and the private sector. Because of the lack of data available on m-FS, transaction limits were rarely set as a result of risk-based analysis. Limits for m-BSA transactions were arbitrarily put at similar levels as those for other channels, such as ATMs or the Internet (see Table 11). Korean authorities however, have developed a way to determine limits on m-BSA trans-actions based on statistical evidence (see Box 4).

Mitigation Using Customer Profiling

Customer profiling to prevent fraud was observed as the key reason for setting individ-ual transactions limits. For example, wealthy clients are more likely to be given higher transaction limits than poor customers based on usual business conducted by both client segments. Individual clients may also play a role in this. While maximum limits may be prescribed by regulations, innovative practices at certain banks allow their cus-tomer to determine lower limits than required by regulation.[115] For instance, a customer concerned about how much money could be lost if a debit card or mobile phone is stolen may determine their own daily/transactional limits according to individual lev-els of comfort. These practices could be the base for AML and CFT mitigation response for this risk.

---

115. HSBC Brazil.

Table 11. Observed Limits on m-FS Transactions, USD (2007)

	South Africa[1]	Philippines[1]	Brazil[2]	Malaysia	Hong Kong SAR of China	Macao SAR of China	Korea, Rep. of
Limits per transaction	714	—	550–5,500	150 (m-money)	Varies by bank and whether transfer is within same bank	Varies by bank and whether transfer is within same bank	Transaction size triggering extra security features— see Box 4.
Daily in/out limit	714	800[2]	550–5,500	150 (m-money)	—	—	
Monthly in/out limit	3,570	2,000	—	—	—	—	
Maximum balance	3,570	2,000	n.a.	150 (m-money)	130 (stored value card)	130 (stored value card)	

[1] Not predetermined by regulation; derived from customer profiling, registration requirements and type of services.

[2] Lower, US$ 200, self-imposed limit by one provider for its retail customer base.

Sources: FICA Act, Exception 17, Vol. 473 Pretoria, 19 November 2004, No. 27011, http://www.fic.gov.za/info/Revised%20exemption%2017%20+%202nd% 20reporting%20exemption.pdf; http://www.bnm.gov.my/index.php?ch=14. Also, personal interviews at Central Bank of the Philippines; Bank Negara Malaysia; Banco do Brasil; Caixa Economica; Itau; Bradesco; HSBC Brasil; and Claro.

Mitigating the Elusiveness Risk by Using Rules for Monitoring

Customer profiling does not require sophisticated software, so certain suspicious activity was identified by introducing basic filters in the systems of financial institutions. A red flag can be raised in a number of instances that suggest that m-FS is being misused. For example: (i) when the frequency and amounts of transactions in a new m-BSA account go beyond the typical transactions of the customer; (ii) when an m-FS transaction over a certain amount is conducted using an m-BSA account that has never been used; (iii) when the frequency of transactions made during a specific period of time sharply increases in comparison with the typical case, or finally, (iv) when the transaction amount grows beyond the normal case.

Mitigation Through Integrated Internal Controls

m-BSA transactions are usually conducted in real time, which makes them very difficult to monitor. Users can initiate m-BSA transactions at any time. All stages of the transaction occur in fractions of a second, including: sending instruction from mobile phone through the wireless network (SMS, or other technology) to the m-BSA provider, authentication of the user, accessing the account, processing the transaction, and the transaction clearance

---

Box 10: Korean Rules for Detecting m-BSA Suspicious Transactions

According to the Korea Federation of Banks (KFB), the use of mobile phones creates inherent ML and TF risks related to fund transfer, foreign currency exchange and remittances. The following is an example of specific rules used by Korean banks for identifying suspicious transactions (requirements may be different among banks):

- When the same person conducts financial transactions worth more than W 50 million (more than W 10 million per transaction) more than 3 times. (individual).
- When the same person conducts financial transactions worth more than W 100 million (more than W 10 million per transaction) more than 3 times. (juridical person).
- When an account is used for conducting more than 50 cases of deposit/withdrawal transactions for 10 business days.
- When deposit/withdrawal transactions worth more than W 20 million are made via an account that has not been used for 6 months.
- When a customer conducts deposit/withdrawal transactions worth more than W 50 million per day with the closing balance of less than W 100,000.
- When a customer conducts transactions (deposit/payment) more than 100 times via a demand deposit account within a month of opening an account.
- When a customer conducts transactions (deposit/payment) worth more than W 300 million via a demand deposit account within 10 days of opening an account.
- When a beneficial owner is suspected by a financial institution, as in the case of minors conducting transactions worth W 30 million.

When an enhanced risk-based CDD framework is enacted in Korea in 2008, money laundering risks will be measured by customer and scope of transactions, and be assessed in advance.

Source: Korea Federation of Banks (KFB) 2007.

and settlement.[116] The rapidity of this transaction does not give financial institutions enough time to suspend a suspicious transaction until more information is obtained.

Integrated internal controls were observed to manage risks of real time mobile transactions. The same technology that enables m-FS was used by providers to diminish their exposure to risk. Unlike using only manual controls, which usually require time and recurring human intervention, banks, TelCos and other m-BSA providers enhance manual controls with automated controls embedded in their IT systems. Providers noted that these controls need to be set in the IT systems and reviewed (for design and operational effectiveness) on a regular basis. Clear lines of responsibility were established to prevent automated controls from being changed by unauthorized individuals. Finally, providers aimed to make their internal controls systems subject to both internal and external audits conducted in accordance with international IT standards. This last point helps to ensure that the business itself is sound.

---

116. See CGAP for an overview of m-FS technology solutions: http://cgap.org/portal/binary/com .epicentric.contentmanagement.servlet.ContentDeliveryServlet/Technology/docs/M-bankingTechnologies .pdf.

Mitigation Measures
for m-Money

This Appendix describes the main mitigation responses observed for m-Money and comprises the following sections:

- Mitigation responses for Elusiveness
- Mitigation responses for Elusiveness in cross-border remittances

Mitigation Responses for Elusiveness

A centralized registry of account holders to prevent abuse of users with multiple m-Money accounts was being contemplated in some jurisdictions. Through a central repository, TelCos and regulators would view suspicious activity by transfers associated with a name, not solely an account number. Presuming there are sufficient controls to mitigate anonymity risks, law enforcement and TelCos could use this database to find multiple accounts tied to the same user. This would help hinder criminal efforts to conceal the origins of funds by taking advantage of the lack of information shared within the industry.

Authorities can give guidelines to non-bank m-FS providers directly to ensure that they are aware of their AML and CFT obligations. In one jurisdiction, it was observed that the central bank contacted non-banks that were participating in m-Money services to inform them of their obligations under the AML and CFT regime. This would help to close any holes in the regime due to provider unawareness.

Mitigation Responses for Elusiveness and Cross-border Remittances

Strong foreign exchange controls impede m-Money from being used for remittances to foreign recipients. It was observed that barring m-Money from being used in international remittances was a response to diminish the ML and TF risk. Limiting the channels through which money can be sent overseas is a way to preclude it from money laundering or terrorist financing.[117]

Registration for cross-border m-Money providers was required in some jurisdictions in order to diminish risk of abuse. Hong Kong SAR of China requires that TelCos that supply international m-Money services register as RSPs.[118] In other jurisdictions this was enhanced by requiring providers to be licensed. For example, in Malaysia it was observed that entities wishing to provide m-Money needed to do so as e-Money issuers, and as such had to address the central bank's requirements for entering this market. Licenses are granted based on the petitioner's financial history and strength, company governance, customer protection rules, safety of the proposed e-money system and background information on shareholders and managers. After approval is granted, the FIU notifies the new m-Money issuer of its AML and CFT obligations.

---

117. This method has consequences in terms of financial inclusion.
118. Although it was also observed that there are no fit and proper checks and no information about the beneficial owners of the company.

The Financial Action Task Force (FATF)

Since its creation, the FATF[119] has spearheaded the effort to adopt and implement measures designed to counter the use of the financial system by criminals. It established a series of Recommendations in 1990, and revised them in 1996 and 2003 to ensure that they remain up to date and relevant to evolving ML threats. The Recommendations set out the basic framework for AML and CFT efforts and are intended to be for universal application.

In response to mounting concern over ML, the FATF was established by the G-7 Summit held in Paris in 1989. Recognizing the threat posed to the banking system and to financial institutions, the G-7 Heads of State, or Government and President of the European Commission, convened a task force from the G-7 member States, the European Commission, and eight other countries.

The task force was given the responsibility of examining ML techniques and trends, reviewing actions already taken at national and international levels, and setting out measures still needing to be taken to combat ML. In April 1990, less than one year after its creation, the FATF issued a report containing a set of 40 Recommendations, which provide a comprehensive plan of action needed to fight against ML.

During 1991 and 1992, the FATF expanded its membership from its original 16 to 28 members. In 2000, the FATF expanded to 31 members, in 2003 to 33 members, and in 2007, it expanded to its current 34 members. The FATF has continued to examine the methods used to launder criminal proceeds and has completed two rounds of mutual

---

119. Information on this page has been adapted from "About the FATF" at www.fatf-gafi.org.

evaluations of its member countries and jurisdictions. A third round of mutual evaluations has commenced.

It has also updated the 40 Recommendations to reflect the changes which have occurred in money laundering and has sought to encourage other countries around the world to adopt anti-money laundering measures. In 2001, the development of standards in the fight against terrorist financing was added to the mission of the FATF. As a result, the FATF issued a set of special recommendations to combat terrorist financing. See the FATF website at www.fatf-gafi.org for further information.

Overview of m-FS Risk Identification and Mitigation

Observed ML and TF Risk Factors

Perceived Risks	Observed Types of Risk	m-fINFO	m-BSA	m-Payment	m-Money	Key Control Measures
Anonymity Fake Identification Pooling and Delegation	Anonymity	Low	Acquisition of customers by off-branch or non-face-to-face transactions possible. Unauthorized use of an existing m-BSA services through phone theft, passing on of a phone or a breach in the wireless network.	Risks observed for m-BSA services	Risks observed for m-BSA services	Innovative KYC Procedures Advanced identification mechanisms
Smurfing	Elusiveness	Low	Use of mobile phone at the layering stage of the ML process	Risks observed for m-BSA services	Risks observed for m-BSA services Multiple m-Money accounts Cross-border mobile remittances	Limits on transactions Customer profiling Monitoring Reporting
Rapidity	Rapidity	Low	Rapidity of m-FS transactions	Risks observed for m-BSA services	Risks observed for m-BSA services	Integrated system of internal controls Managing risk of 3rd party service providers
m-FS Providers Falling Outside the Regulations	Poor oversight	Low	Oversight loopholes for bank m-FS providers	Oversight of banks' role in non-bank m-FS models Poor regulation and AML and CFT supervision of non-bank m-FS providers	Oversight of banks' role in non-bank m-FS models Poor regulation and AML and CFT supervision of non-bank m-FS providers m-FS shell companies	Guidelines on m-BSA and risk management Ensuring that non-bank m-FS providers are regulated, licensed and supervised.

Glossary

Bilateral Remittance Corridor Analysis—The Financial Market Integrity Unit (FPDFI) of the World Bank has conducted a series of studies to expand existing knowledge on workers' remittances to developing countries, with a view to developing best practices on options to protect the integrity of remittance markets, while improving efficiency and transparency of transfer channels for remittance flows, and promoting access to financial services for both remittance senders and recipients.

Churn Rate—The percentage of customers who end their relationship with a company in a given time period. Churn rate typically applies to subscription services, such as long-distance phone service or magazines.

Customer Detail Record—Computer record containing data unique to a specific call related to a mobile operator's recent system usage such as the identities of sources (points of origin), the identities of destinations (end points), the duration of each call, and the amount billed for each call.

Customer Due Diligence—Processes that include verifying a customer's identity and assessing the risks associated with that customer which enable the financial institution or another entity to predict with relative certainty the types of transactions in which a customer is likely to engage. These processes assist the bank in determining when transactions are potentially suspicious.

Electronic Currency—see e-Money.

e-Money—Short for electronic money. A stored-value or prepaid product in which a record of the funds or value available to the consumer for multipurpose use, including transfers to other users and conversion to and from cash, is stored on an electronic device in the consumer's possession. Common uses are phone credits and airtime as tender that users can trade for other goods and services.

FATF-styled Regional Bodies—The FSRB bodies work to assess and facilitate the implementation of the FATF 40+9 Recommendations in their region.

Financial Action Task Force—An inter-governmental body whose purpose is the development and promotion of national and international policies to combat money laundering and terrorist financing. The FATF is therefore a "policy-making body" created in 1989 that works to generate the necessary political will to bring about legislative and regulatory reforms in these areas. The FATF published the 40 + 9 Recommendations in order to meet this objective.

Financial Intelligence Unit—A central, national agency responsible for receiving (and as permitted, requesting), analyzing and disseminating to the competent authorities, disclosures of financial information: (i) concerning suspected proceeds of crime and potential financing of terrorism, or (ii) required by national legislation or regulation, in order to combat money laundering and terrorism financing.

Know-Your-Customer—The due diligence and bank regulation that financial institutions and other regulated entities must perform to identify their clients and ascertain relevant information pertinent to doing financial business with them.

Mobile Banking and Securities Account—An electronic channel to access financial services for bank/securities account holders to execute financial transactions through their mobile phone.

Mobile Financial Information Services—A means through which users may access data related to their personal accounts and/or general financial information on a mobile telephone.

Mobile Money—The value stored on a mobile phone or associated with a mobile phone account for the purpose of issuance, intermediation, multi-purpose use and redemption of electronic money.

Mobile Payment Services—A service that allows non-bank/securities account holders to use a mobile phone for making payments. This is carried through either a bank or non-bank entity (for example, a credit card company, mobile operator) and not based on a pre-existing bank/securities account.

Mobile Financial Services—The use of financial services through means unique to a mobile telephone.

Near Field Communications—A standards-based, short-range wireless connectivity technology that enables simple and safe two-way interactions among electronic devices. Can be used for POS transactions through an NFC-equipped mobile phone.

Non-bank Financial Institutions—Remittance service providers, microfinance institutions, and telecommunications companies.

Point of Sale—The physical location where a sale is completed. Usually used as "POS terminal" to refer to the credit card terminal (equipment).

Remittance Service Providers—Bank and non-bank entities that provide value transfer services both domestically and internationally.

Short Message Service—Short text messages that can be sent to and from a mobile phone.

Subscriber Identification Module—the smart card necessary for the operation of most mobile phones. Is used as one of the technologies in m-FS.

Suspicious Transaction Report—If a financial institution notes something suspicious about a transaction or activity, it may file a report with the FIU that will analyze it and cross check it with other information. The information on an STR varies by jurisdiction.

Bibliography

ABA (American Bankers Association). Undated. "Safety and Soundness: Operational Risk in the Era of Basel II." *ABA Banking* 65, Special section.

Asian Banker. 2007. "Upwardly Mobile." *70* (15 August).

BSP (Bangko Sentral ng Pilipinas). 2007a. *Circular 2*. Manilla, Philippines: Bangko Sentral ng Pilipinas.

————. 2007b. *Circular 4*. Manilla, Philippines: Bangko Sentral ng Pilipinas.

Basel Committee on Banking Supervision-BIS. 2001a. Customer Due Diligence for Banks, http://www.bis.org/publ/bcbs77.htm.

————. 2001b. Risk Management Principles for Electronic Banking http://www.bis.org/publ/bcbs82.htm.

Bester, Hennie, Doubell Chamberlain, Louis de Koker, Christine Hougaard, Ryan Short, Anja Smith, and Richard Walker. Forthcoming. "Implementing FATF Standards in Developing Countries and Financial Inclusion: Findings and Guidelines." Washington, D.C.: Genesis Analytics (Pty) Ltd. funded by the FIRST Initiative.

Butler, Mark, and Rachelle Boyle. 2003. *Alternative Remittance Regulation and Implementation Package.* Asia-Pacific Group Typologies Working Group on Alternative Remittance & Underground Banking Systems. Sydney.

CGAP (Consultant Group to Assist the Poor). 2006. Use of Agents in Branchless Banking for The Poor: Rewards, Risks, And Regulation. Focus Note 38. Washington, D.C.

————. 2007. Notes on Regulation of Branchless Banking in Kenya. November. http://cgap.org/portal/binary/com.epicentric.contentmanagement.servlet.ContentDeliveryServlet/Documents/Kenya-Notes-On-Regulation-Branchless-Banking-2007.pdf (accessed December 19, 2007).

————. [Forthcoming]. Focus Note No. 41 [on regulation of branchless banking]. Washington, D.C.

Chatain, Pierre-Laurent. 2004. "The World Bank's Role in the Fight Against Money Laundering and Terrorist Financing." *Journal of the International Law Association* International Law Forum 6 (3–4).

Christen, Robert Peck, Richard Rosenberg, and Veena Jayadeva. 2004. "Financial Institutions with a "Double Bottom Line": Implications for the Future of Microfinance." Occasional Paper 8, Consultant Group to Assist the Poor, Washington, D.C.

Chipchase, Jan. 2007. "Connections & Consequences, Insight & Innovation: Why the Humble Mobile Phone is Universally Popular across Cultures." Paper presented at the International Finance Corporation, Washington, D.C.

Commission Staff. 2006. Working Document on the Review of the E-Money Directive (2000/46/EC), Brussels, 19.07.2006 SEC, 1049.

De Luna, José, Raúl Hernández-Coss, Kamil Borowik, and Federico Lagi. 2006. "The Italy-Albania Remittance Corridor: Shifting from the Physical Transfer of Cash to a Formal

Money Transfer System." The World Bank, Washington, D.C. http://siteresources
.worldbank.org/INTAML/Resources/2006_World_Bank_Italy_Albania_Remittance_
Corridor.pdf.

Demetis, Dionysios S., and Bernard W. Dyer. 2006. Paper Interview. London School of
Economics, Department of Management, Information Systems Group. http://
personal.lse.ac.uk/demetis/PaperInterview.pdf (accessed August 20, 2007).

Ehrenfeld, Rachel, and John Wood. 2007a. "How Terrorists Send Money." United Press
International. May 1, 2007. http://www.spacewar.com/reports/How_Terrorists_Send_
Money_999.html (accessed August 20, 2007).

———. 2007b. "Terrorist Funding in Real Time." *American Thinker.* April 11. http://www
.americanthinker.com/2007/04/terrorist_funding_in_real_time.html (accessed August 20,
2007).

Epper Hoffman, Karen. 2007. "Mobile Banking: Where's the Business Case?" *BAI (Banking
Administration Institute)* 83(5). http://www.bai.org/bankingstrategies/2007-sep-oct/
Mobile_Banking/ (accessed March 10, 2008).

Financial Action Task Force (FATF). 2003. "The 40 Recommendations." http://www.fatf-
gafi.org/document/28/0,3343,en_32250379_32236930_33658140_1_1_1_1,00.html#
40recs (accessed February 14, 2008).

———. 2006a. "Methodology for Assessing Compliance with the FATF 40 Recommendations and the FATF 9 Special Recommendations." Paris. http://www.fatf-gafi.org/
dataoecd/14/53/38336949.pdf.

———. 2006b. "Report on New Payment Methods." Paris. http://www.fatf-gafi.org/dataoecd/
30/47/37627240.pdf.

———. 2007. "Guidance on the Risk-Based Approach to Combating Money Laundering
and Terrorist Financing: High Level Principles and Procedures." Guidance Paper. Paris.

GSMA (GSM Association). 2006a. "GSM Hits Two Billion Milestone." Press Release. 16 June.

———. 2006b. *Universal Access Report.* London. http://www.gsmworld.com/documents/
universal_access_full_report.pdf (accessed January 3, 2008).

Hernández-Coss, Raúl. 2005. *The US-Mexico Remittance Corridor: Lessons on Shifting from
Informal to Formal Transfer Systems.* World Bank Working Paper No. 47. Washington,
D.C.: The World Bank.

———. 2007. "The Perception of Money Laundering Risks and the Use of New Technologies: The Case of m-Transactions." Presentation to the Conference on Next Gen-
eration Access to Finance: Gaining Scale and Reducing Costs with Technology and
Credit Scoring. Washington, D.C.

Isern, Jennifer, David Porteous, Raúl Hernández-Coss, and Chinyere Egwuagu. 2005. *AML/
CFT Regulation: Implications for Financial Service Providers that Serve Low-Income People.*
Focus Note No. 29. Washington: Consultative Group to Assist the Poor and World
Bank. July.

ITU (International Telecommunications Union). 2005. *International Telecommunications.*
Geneva: ITU.

———. 2007. *Global Trends in Telecommunications,* 7. Geneva.

Ivatury, Gautum, and Mark Pickens. 2006. *Mobile Phone Banking and Low-Income Customers:
Evidence from South Africa.* Washington, DC: Consultative Group to Assist the Poor.

Kim, Jabonn. 2006. *Recent Development of Electronic Finance and Major Issues for Further
Development.* Seoul: Korea Institute of Finance.

Krebs, Brian. 2007. "Terrorism's Hook into Your Inbox: U.K. Case Shows Link Between Online Fraud and Jihadist Networks." *Washington Post* Online. July 5. http://www .washingtonpost.com/wp-dyn/content/article/2007/07/05/AR2007070501153_pf.html (accessed November 9, 2007).

Krishna, R. Jai. 2006. "Post Offices to Check Mobile User's ID." Cybermedia India Online Limited. http://www.ciol.com/content/news/2006/106100308.asp (accessed August 20, 2007).

Littlefield, Elizabeth, Brigit Helms, and David Porteous. 2006. *Financial Inclusion 2015: Four Scenarios for the Future of Microfinance.* Focus Note No. 39. Washington, DC: Consultant Group to Assist the Poor. October.

Lyman, Timothy, Mark Pickens, and David Porteous. 2008. "Regulating Transformational Branchless Banking: Mobile Phones and Other Technology to Increase Access to Finance." Focus Note No. 43. Consultant Group to Assist the Poor, Washington, D.C.

Monilink. 2007. "RBS Mobile Phone Banking Coming Soon" http://monilink.co.uk/banks/ royal-bank-of-scotland/ (accessed September 7, 2007).

Porteous, David. 2006. *The Enabling Environment for Mobile Banking in Africa.* Department for International Development.

Porteous, David, and Neville Wishart. 2006. "m-Banking: A Knowledge Map." Washington, DC: infoDev / World Bank. http://www.infodev.org/en/Publication.169.html.

SBP (State Bank of Pakistan). 2007. "Policy Paper on Regulatory Framework for Mobile Banking in Pakistan." Draft Policy Paper. Banking Policy & Regulations Department. Islamabad, Pakistan. http://www.sbp.org.pk/bprd/2007/Policy_Paper_RF_Mobile_ Banking_07-Jun-07.pdf. Accessed August 20, 2007.

Schott, Paul Allan. 2006. *Reference Guide to Anti-Money Laundering and Combating the Financing of Terrorism,* 2nd Ed. Washington, D.C: The World Bank and International Monetary Fund.

Teves, Oliver. 2007. "Allowance Made Simple for Filipinos." *Express.* October 10.

Todor, Nancy. 2007. "Global Remittances: New Initiatives in M-banking—The Citigroup-Vodafone Partnership." Presentation to World Bank/IFC Conference on "Exploring Frontiers in Payments Systems Development," Washington, D.C., May 31. http://info. worldbank.org/etools/library/latestversion.asp?240413.

Trucano, Michael. 2006. "m-banking, m-remittances: Case Studies from the Philippines." Presentation to the Nigeria Financial System Strategy Workshop, Washington, D.C., December 19. http://siteresources.worldbank.org/INTAFRSUMAFTPS/Resources/m-banking_m-remittances_case_studies_from_the_Philippines(MT).pdf.

Vodafone Group Plc. 2007. "Moving the Debate Forward." Policy Paper Series No. 6.

Wishart, Neville. 2006. "Micro-Payment Systems and Their Application to Mobile Net-works." InfoDev, January. http://www.infodev.org/en/Publication.43.html (accessed March 8, 2008).

Wikipedia. 2007. "Smurfing" en.wikipedia.org/wiki/Smurfing_(crime) (accessed October 2, 2007).

Wireless Intelligence. http://www.wirelessintelligence.com (accessed August 13, 2007).

World Bank. 2006. *Financial Sector Development Indicators.* Washington, D.C.

———. 2007. *Finance for All? Policies and Pitfalls in Expanding Access.* Policy Research Report. Washington, D.C.

Author Biographies

Pierre-Laurent Chatain joined the World Bank's Financial Market Integrity Unit in September 2002 as Senior Financial Sector Specialist. He has led several anti-money laundering assessment missions as part of the Financial Sector Assessment Program in Anglophone, Francophone, and Spanish speaking countries, and designed and delivered many technical assistance programs and outreach events in Africa, the Middle-East, and Latin America. Before joining the World Bank, Mr. Chatain worked for the Bank of France for more than 15 years. He held several positions in succession within the legal and inspection departments. He was auditor from 1992 to 1996, then was promoted to inspector. He also served as mission chief at the French Banking Commission where he led multi-disciplinary on-site inspection teams in commercial banks in France and overseas. He also exercised managerial responsibilities at the Bank of France as Deputy-Director of the On-site Control Department. Mr. Chatain has published widely on issues of mediation, conflict resolutions, and civil bankruptcy. He is a graduate of the French Political Science Institute.

Raúl Hernández-Coss has been the primary task manager for the development of Bilateral Remittance Corridor Analysis (BRCA), which is aimed at supporting countries on strengthening their remittances systems and promoting a shift from informal to formal fund transfer (FFT) systems. His work on remittances has supported regional efforts directed towards analyzing remittance markets and has engaged donors on promoting financial literacy and migrant access to formal funds transfer systems. His work has also helped design effective policy avenues aimed at enhancing partnerships between remittance sending and recipient countries. As part of the Bank's legal department, Mr. Hernández-Coss contributed to the review of central banks and banking laws to determine the effectiveness of the legal framework in ensuring a sound banking system. His analysis has also helped determine the adequacy of the Bank's exit framework and deposit insurance system. Mr. Hernández-Coss has worked with the Consultative Group to Assist the Poor (CGAP) on the first analysis of AML and CFT regulations and their implications for financial service providers that serve low-income people. He graduated with a Law degree from Instituto Tecnológico Autónomo de México (ITAM), a Masters of International Affairs from Columbia University, and a Masters of Law from Georgetown University.

Kamil Borowik, as a Financial Analyst in the World Bank's Financial and Private Sector Development Network, focused on risk management, capital market development, and access to finance through bank and non-bank financial institutions. Since the organization of the 2006 International Conference on Migrant Remittances and Access to Finance, he expanded the World Bank's interest in exploring technology as safe and sustainable means to develop access to financial services. He has spearheaded this work since its conception, and participated in the entire fieldwork related to this study. Before joining the World

Bank, he was a Senior Consultant at KPMG Advisory Services focusing on enterprise risk management, management information systems, and project management engagements in financial services. Mr. Borowik graduated with a masters in Corporate Finance from the Cracow University of Economics, Erasmus Socrates scholarship at the University of Greenwich, UK and the Vanderbilt University-BAI Postgraduate School of Bank Operations, Payments and Technology.

Andrew Zerzan analyzes technology as a key driver for sustainable economic development. At the World Bank, his work focuses on new innovations and their role in promoting access to financial services and market integrity. In 2006, Mr. Zerzan initiated published research on information and communication technologies for economic development at the World Bank Institute. His analysis has gauged the effectiveness of national and international regimes to mitigate the risks of growth, such as illicit money flows, terrorist financing, and money laundering. Mr. Zerzan draws on his private sector experience as a consultant in Japan where he built a grassroots business that has bridged disparities in strategic communications among global companies. He was educated in the United Kingdom, Spain, Canada and the United States.

Eco-Audit

Environmental Benefits Statement

The World Bank is committed to preserving Endangered Forests and natural resources. We print World Bank Working Papers and Country Studies on 100 percent postconsumer recycled paper, processed chlorine free. The World Bank has formally agreed to follow the recommended standards for paper usage set by Green Press Initiative—a nonprofit program supporting publishers in using fiber that is not sourced from Endangered Forests. For more information, visit www.greenpressinitiative.org.

In 2007, the printing of these books on recycled paper saved the following:

Trees*	Solid Waste	Water	Net Greenhouse Gases	Total Energy
264	12,419	96,126	23,289	184 mil.
'40' in height and 6–8" in diameter	Pounds	Gallons	Pounds CO_2 Equivalent	BTUs

green press INITIATIVE